EVALUATING TEACHERS OF MUSIC PERFORMANCE GROUPS

David I   ksen

Published in Partnership with MENC: The National Association for Music Education

ROWMAN & LITTLEFIELD EDUCATION

Lanham • New York • Toronto • Plymouth, UK

Published in the United States of America
by Rowman & Littlefield Education
A Division of Rowman & Littlefield Publishers, Inc.
A wholly owned subsidiary of The Rowman & Littlefield Publishing Group, Inc.
4501 Forbes Boulevard, Suite 200, Lanham, Maryland 20706
www.rowmaneducation.com

Estover Road
Plymouth PL6 7PY
United Kingdom

British Library Cataloguing in Publication Information Available

Library of Congress Cataloging-in-Publication Data

Doerksen, David P.
   Evaluating teachers of music performance groups / David P. Doerksen.
      p. cm.
   Rev. ed. of: Guide to evaluating teachers of music performance groups. c1990.
   "Published in partnership with MENC: The National Association for Music
Education"
   Includes bibliographical references (p. 85).
   ISBN-13: 978-1-57886-441-6 (pbk. : alk. paper)
   ISBN-10: 1-57886-441-0 (pbk. : alk. paper)
   1. School music—Instruction and study. 2. Music teachers—Rating of—United
States. I. Doerksen, David P. Guide to evaluating teachers of music performance
groups. II. MENC: The National Association for Music Education (U.S.) III. Title.

MT1.D64 2006
780.71—dc22   2006011686

∞™ The paper used in this publication meets the minimum requirements of
American National Standard for Information Sciences—Permanence of Paper
for Printed Library Materials, ANSI/NISO Z39.48-1992.
Manufactured in the United States of America.

Contents

Appendixes

List of Figures, Tables, and Forms

Foreword

THE FIRST EDITION OF *Evaluating Teachers of Music Performance Groups* was an instant success. Countless teachers and supervisors were grateful to see the publication of a book that combined careful research and practical experience. There was no shortage of books on the subject of evaluating teachers, but no one had set forth such direct tenets of mentoring, coaching, and nurturing music teachers, and leaders of performance groups in particular.

Evaluating music teachers and leaders of performance groups is still a critical activity in ensuring a high-quality music program. Rather than just reprinting the first edition when they ran low on stock, MENC (the National Association for Music Education) wisely contacted Dr. Doerksen about doing a comprehensive update.

This has worked out very well. The book still fills an important niche—and Dr. Doerksen's continued interest in the topic, additional research, and applied experience make this new edition meritorious.

Make no mistake about it: This is a book about school leadership, because successful evaluation is part of good leadership. A book like this one is not only useful but necessary. The call for research-based practices has never been stronger. When Dr. Doerksen authored the first edition, the standards movement was in its infancy. Now the National Standards for Music Education are widely studied and applied. Compelling research exists on the characteristics of effective teaching; much research on the importance of mentoring and a wealth of evidence show that high-quality teachers reflect their modeling and incisive, targeted coaching. The best supervisors and the most appreciative teachers have always understood the role of effective evaluation.

Evaluating Teachers of Music Performance Groups provides a practical outline as well as guidance for teachers and administrators who face the daily challenges of building a quality music program. Teachers have as much vested interest in their programs as their supervisors and principals. Evaluation that identifies areas where teachers need to grow, and that provides assistance and guided practice for such growth, benefits children and music students at every level.

For those supervisors who want to examine their own leadership challenges more closely, I would refer them to the Mid-continent Research for Education and Learning's (McREL's) Balanced Leadership Profile 360. But no matter whether the music supervisor is still something of a novice or is very experienced, the most important thing that he or she can do is get into the classroom with open eyes and ears, with a rubric that is understandable to the teacher as well as the supervisor. In the final analysis, as Dr. Doerksen makes wonderfully clear, there is no substitute for guided observation and a follow-up conversation in which both the teacher and the supervisor collaborate and contribute.

The effective music educator seeks constantly to improve his or her skills, teaching methodologies, and knowledge of repertoire. Through the collaborative process that this book encourages, educators will improve both their teaching and music programs. We are all grateful to both MENC and Dr. Doerksen for publishing an updated second edition of *Evaluating Teachers of Music Performance Groups.*

—LARRY D. WILLIAMS
Superintendent of Schools, Sioux City, Iowa
Former President, NW Division, MENC
Lowell Mason Fellow

Introduction

SINCE THE PUBLICATION OF *A Nation at Risk* (National Commission on Excellence in Education 1983), there have been omnipresent calls for sweeping change and reform in education. The ink is hardly dry on one innovation before another one comes along. New national and state standards are now in place, and high-stakes testing is underway at state and national levels. Even so, accountability is still an issue, and the success of any reform effort is dependent on the quality of our teachers.

In 1996, the National Commission on Teaching and America's Future proposed that "within a decade—by the year 2006—we will provide every student in America with what should be his or her educational birthright: access to competent, caring, qualified teaching" (p. 21). The year 2006 is here, and most observers would agree that we are still a long way from this goal, and that high-quality teacher evaluation is a must if we are to reach it. Unfortunately, as Stronge and Tucker (2003) have stated, "Teacher evaluation has been viewed not as a vehicle for growth and improvement, but rather as a formality—a superficial function that has lost its meaning. When school principals and other evaluators approach education as a mechanical exercise and teachers view it as an event that must be endured, evaluation becomes little more than a time-consuming charade" (p. 6).

Indeed, music teacher evaluation has been fraught with problems. Individuals with responsibility for evaluating music instruction—whether general administrators or music supervisors—are seldom prepared to do a high-quality job. The general administrator is trained, if at all, to focus on a set of generic behaviors such as presenting the subject matter clearly, keeping students on task, showing enthusiasm, and directing teaching to an objective. These administrators are usually satisfied with the program if students are under control and actively participating. Such administrators often state with confidence that "I may not know much about music, but I know good teaching when I see it." Still, because they are generalists, they can do little to evaluate instruction in subjects such as music.

The checklists they so often use are of little help. An administrator armed with a checklist once gave a music teacher low marks on "provides for individual differences." When asked the reason for this, the administrator replied that the teacher had insisted that all students tune to the same pitch without making allowances for individual differences. Unless administrators can recognize the difference between excellence and mediocrity in performance, can tell the difference between good and bad tone quality or intonation, or can tell when instructional feedback is appropriate or inappropriate, there is no way a valid professional evaluation can be made.

To be sure, too much is expected of the general administrator. Administration is a tough job, and no individual can be expected to be knowledgeable about each of the many subjects in the curriculum. Mistakes in judgment are easy to make. A foreign language teacher, for example, could be rated by an administrator as a superior instructor, based on high marks in enthusiasm, clarity, classroom control, and active student participation. Yet the students of this same teacher could be learning shocking mispronunciations identifiable only by someone who knows the language. By the same token, a music teacher may be rated highly in the same general areas of enthusiasm, clarity, and classroom control, have large numbers of actively participating students, and still have a group that plays or sings with poor intonation, balance, and tone quality.

An administrator would never think of giving a good evaluation to a math teacher whose students repeatedly got the answers wrong, even though the students were under control, appeared to be enjoying themselves, and seemed to be having a "positive" experience. The same administrator, however, might give a good evaluation to a music teacher on the basis of good classroom control, high enrollment, and evidence that the students enjoy themselves and have positive experiences—regardless of the quality of individual and group music skills demonstrated.

It is not enough to suggest that the administrator seek the help of someone with expertise in the subject matter at hand. An administrator with such a problem is unlikely to recognize that help is needed. Even if he or she recognizes this need, the likelihood of getting effective help is remote. It takes more than someone generally thought "to know a lot about music." In fact, some of the worst evaluations of music instruction are done by administrators who know a little about music through having participated in performance groups themselves in high school or college. Often, such individuals hold onto their casually formed opinions with bulldog tenacity, and their faith in their own judgments is rarely shaken.

Like general administrators, music supervisors are often unprepared to assume evaluation responsibilities. In many cases they move into supervisory roles directly from teaching without the training required to be effective evaluators. These individuals tend to focus on noninstructional aspects of the supervisor's job, such as scheduling, inventory control, purchasing, budget preparation, and the like. Even though they may have been exemplary teachers in their own right, they find that good instruction is easy to recognize but hard to define.

Arguments sometimes occur as to who—a general administrator or a music supervisor—is better qualified to evaluate teachers of music performance groups. The opinion here is that the question of who does the evaluation is not as important as that it be done well. When one considers that poor teachers are not necessarily protected by the tenure system but by administrators who do not know what to do, do not care, or lack the courage to take action, it becomes clear how important high-quality evaluation is to the future of our music programs.

Unlike most books on the subject of teacher evaluation, which are designed for the general administrator who evaluates teachers of many or all subjects, this book is about evaluating teachers of one subject: music performance. Its approach is based on the belief that while general administrators can evaluate those things common to all classrooms, such as the quality of classroom control, planning, and interaction with students, the evaluation of instruction requires expertise in the subject taught.

Every teacher evaluation system must define the teaching task and provide a mechanism to evaluate the teacher (Darling-Hammond,

1990). Such a system is set forth here. In Part I, the basic documents of an evaluation system are presented. Part II includes additional documents and a review of the evaluation process, with an emphasis on evaluating music instruction. No claim is made that this approach is the only way to evaluate teachers. It is only one way, but a way that works. Most states now have legislated requirements that have been built into local school district evaluation systems. Most of the ideas and procedures in this book can be adapted to almost any of these systems. These materials may also serve as a resource for college courses such as administration and supervision of school music and for courses where undergraduates visit public school music classrooms to observe and analyze instruction. College and university supervisors may adapt the documents and procedures outlined here for their work with student teachers.

Across the country, parents, policymakers, and educators alike are calling for, even demanding, improvement in our schools (Tucker and Stronge 2005). Those responsible for music teacher evaluation must respond by preparing themselves to meet the challenge of this important task.

Endnotes

Darling-Hammond, L. (1990). Teacher evaluation in transition: Emerging roles and evolving methods. In J. Millman & L. Darling-Hammond (Eds.), *The new handbook of teacher evaluation* (pp. 17–32). Newbury Park, CA: Sage.

National Commission on Excellence in Education. (1983). *A nation at risk: The imperative for educational reform.* Washington, DC: Author.

National Commission on Teaching and America's Future. (1996). *What matters most: Teaching for America's future.* New York: Author.

Stronge, J. H., & Tucker, P. D. (2003). *Handbook on teacher evaluation: Assessing and improving performance.* Larchmont, NY: Eye on Education.

Tucker, P. D., & Stronge, J. H. (2005). *Linking teacher evaluation and student learning.* Alexandria, VA: Association for Supervision and Curriculum Development.

I

Basic Documents

I. Overview of the Evaluation Plan

EVALUATION PLANS ARE quite similar from district to district. The sample in figure 1.1 is typical. "Standards" and "Job Descriptions" appear as basic documents, followed by a sequence of evaluation activities. If performance is satisfactory, the plan proceeds to the final written report and then cycles back to the writing of new goals for the ensuing year. If performance is unsatisfactory, a plan of assistance is prescribed. If performance is still unsatisfactory, an intensive plan of assistance is instituted. Successful completion of either plan returns the teacher to the regular cycle. Failure to complete the intensive plan successfully becomes grounds for dismissal.

Outline of the Evaluation Plan

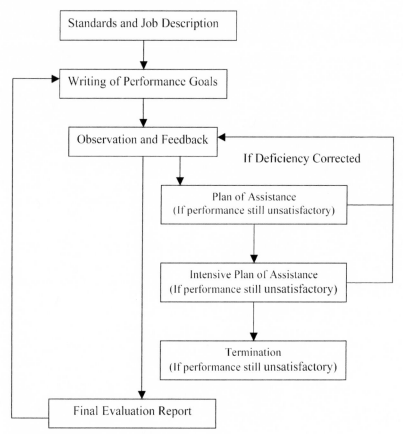

FIGURE 1.1
The Evaluation Plan

The Evaluation Calendar

The evaluation calendar reflects important decisions that have been made in a district with respect to evaluation. Here a supervisor will find answers to questions such as who will be evaluated, and when and how often such evaluations will occur. Without a document of this kind it is impossible to achieve order and control in the evaluation process. With such a calendar, unplanned last-minute observations are avoided and desultory patterns of observations are replaced by systematic, regularly scheduled classroom visits.

On the sample in figure 1.1, both formal and informal evaluations are specified. "Formal evaluation" is used to describe those evaluations that follow the steps of the clinical-supervision model (a pre-observation conference with the teacher, the classroom observation itself, and a post-observation conference). "Informal evaluation" refers to interactions between the supervisor and the teacher, which usually include—but do not require—a classroom visit, and which may or may not be scheduled. An example of an informal evaluation would be a meeting between the supervisor and the teacher to review enrollment figures and instrumentation. As in formal observations, the focus is on the teacher's progress toward performance goals.

If a district does not have an evaluation calendar, the supervisor must design one for his or her own use. Referring to models from other school districts can be helpful, but questions as to who will be observed and how often and when the observations will take place are best decided by those responsible for evaluation efforts at the local level. (In table 1.1,

TABLE 1.1
Evaluation Calendar

Date to Be Completed	First Year Probationary and Temporary	Second and Third Year Probationary	Permanent Evaluation Year	Alternate Year
	Review Goals	Review Goals	Review Goals	Review Goals
October 1	Four observations (two formal; one informal; one by Oct. 15)	Three observations (two formal; one informal; one by Oct. 15)	Two observations (one formal; one informal; one by March 1)	One observation (formal or informal; one by March 1)
February 15	Final evaluation report	Final evaluation report		
March 1	Write performance goals	Write performance goals		
May 1	One observation (formal or informal)	One observation (formal or informal)	Final evaluation report	Final conference to review annual performance goals
May 15			Write performance goals for next year	

note the differences between the schedule of events for probationary and permanent teachers.)

II. Evaluative Criteria

Evaluative criteria comprise behaviors, competencies, and responsibilities related to the teaching-learning process. These criteria are incorporated into standards and job descriptions, two basic documents used for evaluation. For such documents to be valid, it is essential that they draw from the best thinking and research available:

NBPT Standards

A good source of evaluative criteria comes from the work of the National Board for Professional Teaching Standards, an organization established in 1987 to develop standards for teacher certification. The NBPTS has published a set of five "Core Propositions" that define highly qualified teachers in the broadest sense, and can be used as a primary source for developing the evaluative criteria that make up standards and job descriptions (National Board for Professional Teaching Standards, 1994, p. 3–7):

1. Teachers are committed to students and their learning.
2. Teachers know the subjects they teach and how to teach those subjects to students.
3. Teachers are responsible for managing and monitoring student learning.
4. Teachers think systematically about their practice and learn from experience.
5. Teachers are members of learning communities.

Teacher Effectiveness Research

The findings of teacher effectiveness research are a second source of evaluative criteria to be used in standards and job descriptions. This line of research has been the subject of much interest since the 1960s. The part of teacher effectiveness research that attempts to shed light on the relationship between teacher behavior and student achievement has been particularly productive. The findings in this area are a joint yield of many studies in various subjects—mostly math and reading—and tend to confirm commonsense notions about teaching that have been held for a long time.

There is, of course, a need for caution when generalizing findings from studies done in certain subjects and grade levels to other subjects, grade levels, and students. Nevertheless, as Baxter and Stauffer (1988) point out, "to the degree that teaching music is like teaching other subjects, music teachers can learn from that research" (p. 60). The Effective Teacher Profile (see below) includes the findings of teacher effectiveness research that can most readily be generalized to music instruction in performance groups.

According to Grant and Drafall (1991), "Music education researchers, with few exceptions, have not looked to these findings [of teacher effectiveness research] as a relevant source for research ideas or methodology" (p. 44). Duke (1999/2000) reviewed eighty-six studies on teacher effectiveness in music and found that

> only 13 of the 86 investigations measured student achievement. In those instances where aspects of teacher behavior were measured in relation to accomplishment of the learner, the strength of association between the behavior of the teacher and student achievement was found to be either very weak or statistically nonsignificant. (p. 1)

Most teacher effectiveness research in music education is based on contest results or teaching excellence as defined by experts, and it is still to be determined if the teacher characteristics, competencies, and skills identified in these studies have any relationship to student achievement. Until teachers of performance groups agree on what should be taught and begin assessing student achievement, the relationship between student achievement and teacher behaviors will not be confirmed (Grant and Drafall 1991).

Nevertheless, there are findings from research in music education that are consistent with those from other subjects, as, for example, those of Price (1983) on the use of rehearsal time and the importance of student awareness of goals, and those of Sang (1982, 1987) on modeling and diagnosis/prescription. Although this body of research is small, it is important because music performance classrooms and instruction differ in some respects from other instructional settings. The classes are almost always elective and often include from sixty to eighty students, each with an instrument or voice. Instructional materials are for the most part limited to sheet music rather than books. Normal classroom routines such as extended discussions, seat work, and paper-and-pencil tests are seldom used. The vehicle for the delivery of instruction is the rehearsal, in which students are on task and actively participating a high percentage of the time. The mode of student feedback to the instructor (musical performance) is unique, and the amount of that feedback is much higher than the amount of student feedback in most other types of classes.

An Effective Teacher Profile

An Effective Teacher Profile, based on the sources referred to above, is a useful prerequisite to the writing of job descriptions and standards. The items that appear on the Effective Teacher Profile were culled from researchers such as Berliner (1980), Medley (1979), Rosenshine (1979), Brophy and Evertson (1976), and Fisher et al. (1978). An effective teacher:

1. Cares about students and wants to help them learn.
2. Interacts comfortably and frequently with students on instructional activities.
3. Shows enthusiasm.
4. Is academically oriented and has a commitment to academic achievement.
5. Establishes and maintains an orderly and supportive classroom environment with relatively little effort.
6. Provides for a high rate of active student participation, including spending most of class time in performance.
7. Identifies goals, and assesses, keeps track of, and provides feedback promptly and often to students on their progress on instructional tasks
8. Matches activities and materials to individual and group skills and needs.
   a. Diagnoses performance problems accurately as they occur.
   b. Prescribes corrective feedback for problems as they occur.
   c. Makes sure students have thoroughly learned prerequisite skills.

9. Provides for a high rate of student success.
10. Gives clear directions and makes sure students understand what to do before undertaking assignments.
11. Provides time for practice and review, including guided practice.
12. Models effectively.
13. Has a system of rules and procedures that allows students to tend to personal and procedural needs without having to check with the teacher.

III. Standards

Teachers need to be aware of the criteria that will be used to evaluate them. These criteria can be divided into two categories: general and specific. General performance criteria, known as standards, apply to all teachers, regardless of subject or grade level. (*Teachers*, as used here, refers to all nonsupervisory staff licensed by the state.) Specific criteria, when written according to subject and level of instruction, are known as job descriptions. To illustrate the difference between these two types of evaluative criteria, a general criterion in the standards may call for using a variety of instructional techniques, strategies, and materials, while a job description for a music teacher may specify that the teacher design or obtain and use sequences for the teaching of music reading and instrumental or vocal technique. The following sample set of standards is typical:

1. Professional and Personal

1.01 Is current and has depth in learning theory, teaching methods, subject matter, and district curriculum/texts.
1.02 Communicates, cooperates, and works effectively with fellow teachers, administrators, parents, and others.
1.03 Acts in a discreet and professional manner when discussing student or school problems.
1.04 Seeks professional self-improvement activities.
1.05 Has a positive attitude and interest in teaching as a profession.
1.06 Follows specified performance criteria, policies, and procedures of the building and district.

2. Planning

2.01 Continually plans appropriate learning activities of high quality by
     2.01.01 Matching instructional activities and materials to indi-
             vidual and group needs.
     2.01.02 Selecting activities and materials that are clearly related
             to district, school, and/or department objectives.
2.02 Uses granted planning time for tasks related to the instructional
     program.
2.03 Establishes a series of student objectives that are clear and con-
     sistent with adopted curriculum, appropriately sequenced, spe-
     cific, and measurable.

3. Classroom or Activity Management

3.01 Establishes and maintains an orderly and supportive environ-
     ment for students.
3.02 Consistently follows school regulations regarding attendance re-
     porting, grading, and record keeping.
3.03 Demonstrates a courteous and helpful attitude toward students.
3.04 Recognizes conditions that may lead to disciplinary problems
     and takes appropriate preventive action.
3.05 Reinforces desired pupil behaviors and responds appropriately
     to disruptive student behaviors.
3.06 Follows procedures defined in district/building discipline policy.

4. Teaching

4.01 Allocates sufficient time to cover the subject matter, materials,
     or activities.
4.02 Maximizes time when students are paying attention and work-
     ing on tasks directly related to the subject matter, materials, or
     activities.
4.03 Provides time for practice and review as needed.
4.04 Makes sure students understand what to do before undertaking
     assignments.
4.05 Monitors student understanding and adjusts the lesson and ac-
     tivity assignments accordingly.

4.06 Uses a variety of instructional techniques, strategies, and materials appropriate to the lesson or activity.

4.07 Incorporates principles of learning.

4.08 Establishes, communicates, and maintains standards of student achievement based on sound professional judgment.

4.09 Conducts interesting and well-paced classes.

5. Evaluation

5.01 Designs and/or selects a variety of effective evaluative techniques to measure student learning.

5.02 Makes use of student records, parent conferences, counselors, resource specialists, test results, and other diagnostic tools to assess the learning needs and capabilities of individual students.

5.03 Assesses, keeps track of, and provides feedback promptly and often to students on their progress and assignments.

5.04 Uses a grading system that is consistent, fair, and supportable.

IV. Job Descriptions

Job descriptions define expected behaviors and competencies, and, along with standards, help give the supervisor a clear idea of what to look for when evaluating a teacher.

Job descriptions vary from district to district. In some districts they are written according to area of specialty and level of instruction. In contrast, many districts have only one job description titled simply "teacher." This is a generic document applying to teachers of all subjects at all levels.

For those charged with evaluating teachers of music performance groups, a set of job descriptions defining the various types of assignments is most useful. Such a set may include, for example, individual documents for secondary band, secondary choir, secondary orchestra, elementary band, and elementary orchestra. In most cases this set should prove more than adequate to assist supervisors in their evaluation responsibilities. For those who prefer a different combination, the number of documents could be reduced to three—band, orchestra, and choir—or expanded to include separate job descriptions for high school, junior high or middle school, and elementary band, orchestra, and choir.

Job descriptions do more than define the various positions in a music program. They also serve as a primary source for teachers' annual performance goals. They can also play an important role in the hiring process. For example, a teacher new to the district may be presented with a job description at the time of interview so that the district's expectations are clear. At the interview the teacher may be asked for a self-assessment of strengths and weaknesses in terms of the job description. Any identified weaknesses then become the subject of the teacher's first-year performance goals.

A word of caution is in order with respect to job descriptions. These documents often list responsibilities such as "building a program that attracts and holds students" and "selecting and requisitioning required instruments and equipment." Because of conditions in the program, it is sometimes impossible for teachers to meet these responsibilities. Examples of such conditions are unsatisfactory schedules, inadequate funds, and poor feeder programs. If teachers are to be held accountable for program quality, the district must do everything in its power to ensure that conditions make it possible for expectations to be met.

Sample job descriptions are given below for a high school band teacher, high school orchestra teacher, secondary vocal music teacher, middle school instrumental music teacher, elementary band or orchestra teacher, and teacher (a generic job description that covers teachers of all subjects). Notice that each job description, with the exception of the one for generic teacher, includes blank spaces to write in additional items. Such items allow the supervisor to tailor the job to the individual teacher and school. For example, an item on marching band, a music theory class, or a humanities class could be included if desired.

If a district has both written standards and job descriptions, it is important that both documents be used in the evaluation process. In this way a comprehensive evaluation is ensured, because both general and specific criteria are included and all required responsibilities and competencies are covered. One advantage to having both standards and job descriptions is that it becomes possible to spread items over two documents rather than one, reducing the length of the forms and making them easier to use.

Job Description: High School Band Teacher

High School Band Teacher

1. Primary function: Instructs classes in band so that students develop individual and group performance skills and understanding of music.
2. Responsible to: Building principal or music supervisor.
3. Assigned responsibilities:
   3.01 Conducts rehearsals and performances, demonstrating understanding of differences in style among various types of music.
   3.02 Presents performances of high musical quality in which groups are well disciplined and make a good appearance.
   3.03 Uses music of high quality in a variety of types and styles.
   3.04 Builds and maintains a program that attracts and holds at least enough students to perform standard concert band literature with a characteristic ensemble sound and standard instrumentation.
   3.05 Teaches to and assesses specified MENC National Standards for Music.
   3.06 Identifies and diagnoses problems in individual and group performance skills, and prescribes appropriate and effective corrective feedback.
   3.07 Designs or selects and uses planned sequences of instruction for the development of band instrument technique and music reading.
   3.08 Collaborates with other district band instructors to ensure continuity in enrollment from elementary to middle to high school.
   3.09 Selects and requisitions required music, instructional materials, instruments, equipment, and supplies.
   3.10 Ensures that instruments and equipment are properly used, maintained, and stored, and that inventory records are accurate and current.
   3.11 Participates cooperatively in school and districtwide activities.
   Additional responsibilities:
   3.12
   3.13
   3.14

4. Minimum qualifications:
   4.01 Teaching license valid for assignment.
   4.02 Working knowledge of band instruments.
   4.03 Conduct music accurately and expressively with self-confidence.
   4.04 Perform on own instrument to illustrate and demonstrate correct technique, corrective measures, and musical expressiveness.
   4.05 Strong personal musicianship.
   Additional qualifications:
   4.06
   4.07
   4.08
5. Minimum term of employment: Teacher contract.
6. Salary level: Placement on teacher salary schedule.
7. Evaluation: Performance of this job will be evaluated in accordance with the board's policy on evaluation of professional personnel.

Approved by: _____ Date _____
                      (supervisor)

Received by: _____ Date _____
                      (staff member)

Job Description: High School Orchestra Teacher

High School Orchestra Teacher

1. Primary function: Instructs classes in orchestra so that students develop individual and group performance skills and understanding of music.
2. Responsible to: Building principal or music supervisor.
3. Assigned responsibilities:
   3.01 Conducts rehearsals and performances, demonstrating understanding of differences in style among various types of music.
   3.02 Presents performances of high musical quality in which groups are well disciplined and make a good appearance.
   3.03 Uses music of high quality in a variety of types and styles.
   3.04 Builds and maintains a program that attracts and holds at least enough students to perform standard string and chamber orchestra literature with a characteristic ensemble sound and instrumentation (at least four first violins, four second violins, two violas, two cellos, and two basses).
   3.05 Teaches to and assesses specified MENC National Standards for Music.
   3.06 Identifies and diagnoses problems in individual and group performance skills, and prescribes appropriate and effective corrective feedback.
   3.07 Designs or selects and uses planned sequences of instruction so that students acquire skills in string technique and music reading.
   3.08 Collaborates with other district orchestra instructors to ensure continuity in enrollment from elementary to middle to high school.
   3.09 Selects and requisitions required music, instructional materials, instruments, equipment, and supplies.
   3.10 Ensures that instruments and equipment are properly used, maintained, and stored, and that inventory records are accurate and current.
   3.11 Participates cooperatively in school and districtwide activities.
   Additional responsibilities:
   3.12
   3.13
   3.14

4. Minimum qualifications:
    4.01 Teaching license valid for assignment.
    4.02 Working knowledge of orchestral string instruments.
    4.03 Conduct music accurately and expressively with self-confidence.
    4.04 Perform on own instrument to illustrate and demonstrate correct technique, corrective measures, and musical expressiveness.
    4.05 Strong personal musicianship.
    Additional qualifications:
    4.06
    4.07
    4.08
5. Minimum term of employment: Teacher contract.
6. Salary level: Placement on teacher salary schedule.
7. Evaluation: Performance of this job will be evaluated in accordance with the board's policy on evaluation of professional personnel.

Approved by: _____ Date _____
               (supervisor)

Received by: _____ Date _____
               (staff member)

Job Description: Secondary Vocal Music Teacher

Secondary Vocal Music Teacher

1. Primary function: Instructs classes in vocal music so that students develop individual and group performance skills and an understanding of music.
2. Responsible to: Building principal or music supervisor.
3. Assigned responsibilities:
   3.01 Teaches students to sing with well-formed vowels and clear, free, focused, in-tune sound.
   3.02 Conducts rehearsals and performances, demonstrating understanding of differences in style among various types of music.
   3.03 Presents performances of high musical quality in which groups are well disciplined and make a good appearance.
   3.04 Uses music of high quality in a variety of types and styles.
   3.05 Builds and maintains a program that attracts and holds at least enough students to perform the standard literature at the assigned level with a characteristic ensemble sound and balance of parts.
   3.06 Identifies and diagnoses problems in individual and group vocal technique, and prescribes appropriate and effective corrective feedback.
   3.07 Teaches to and assesses specified MENC National Standards for Music.
   3.08 Designs or selects and uses planned sequences of instruction so that students acquire skills in vocal technique and music reading.
   3.09 Selects and requisitions required music, equipment, and supplies.
   3.10 Ensures that music and equipment are properly used, maintained, and stored, and that inventory records are accurate and current.
   3.11 Participates cooperatively in school and districtwide activities.
   Additional Responsibilities:
   3.12
   3.13
   3.14

4. Minimum qualifications:
   4.01 Teaching license valid for assignment.
   4.02 Working knowledge of the voice at the assigned level.
   4.03 Conduct music accurately and expressively with self-confidence.
   4.04 Sing unself-consciously to illustrate and to demonstrate correct technique, corrective measures, and musical expressiveness.
   4.05 Strong personal musicianship.
   Additional qualifications:
   4.06
   4.07
   4.08
5. Minimum term of employment: Teacher contract.
6. Salary level: Placement on teacher salary schedule.
7. Evaluation: Performance on this job will be evaluated in accordance with the board's policy on evaluation of professional personnel.

Approved by: _____ Date _____
                         (supervisor)

Received by: _____ Date _____
                        (staff member)

Job Description: Middle School Instrumental Music Teacher

Middle School Instrumental Music Teacher

1. Primary function: Instructs classes in band or orchestra so that students develop individual and group performance skills.
2. Responsible to: Building principal or music supervisor.
3. Assigned responsibilities:

   3.01 Conducts rehearsals and performances demonstrating understanding of differences in style among various types of music.

   3.02 Presents performances of high musical quality in which groups are well disciplined and make a good appearance.

   3.03 Uses music of high quality in a variety of types and styles.

   3.04 Builds and maintains a program that attracts and holds at least enough students to (a) perform middle school band or orchestra literature with a standard instrumentation and balance of parts, and (b) sustain a standard and balanced instrumentation at the succeeding high school level.

   3.05 Identifies and diagnoses problems in individual and group performance skills, and prescribes appropriate and effective corrective feedback.

   3.06 Designs or selects and uses planned sequences of instruction for the development of instrumental technique and music reading so that students acquire prerequisite skills for the succeeding high school level of instruction.

   3.07 Teaches to and assesses specified MENC National Standards for Music.

   3.08 Collaborates with other district orchestra or band instructors to ensure continuity in enrollment from elementary to middle to high school.

   3.09 Selects and requisitions required music, instructional materials, instruments, equipment, and supplies.

   3.10 Ensures that instruments and equipment are properly used, maintained, and stored, and that inventory records are accurate and current.

   3.11 Participates cooperatively in school and districtwide activities.

   Additional responsibilities:

   3.12

   3.13

   3.14

4. Minimum qualifications:
   4.01 Teaching license valid for assignment.
   4.02 Working knowledge of all band or orchestral string instruments.
   4.03 Conduct music accurately and expressively with self-confidence.
   4.04 Perform on own instrument to illustrate and demonstrate correct technique, corrective measures, and musical expressiveness.
   4.05 Strong personal musicianship.
   Additional qualifications:
   4.06
   4.07
   4.08
5. Minimum term of employment: Teacher contract.
6. Salary level: Placement on teacher salary schedule.
7. Evaluation: Performance of this job will be evaluated in accordance with the board's policy on evaluation of professional personnel.

Approved by: _____ Date _____
                           (supervisor)

Received by: _____ Date _____
                         (staff member)

Job Description: Elementary Band or Orchestra Teacher

Elementary Band or Orchestra Teacher

1. Primary function: Instructs classes in band or orchestra so that students develop skills in instrumental technique and music reading.
2. Responsible to: Building principal or music supervisor.
3. Assigned responsibilities:

   3.01 Recruits and holds a sufficient number of students to sustain a standard and balanced instrumentation for the succeeding middle school instrumental program.

   3.02 Collaborates with other district orchestra or band instructors to ensure continuity in enrollment from elementary to middle school.

   3.03 Collaborates with principals and staffs of assigned buildings to establish a workable class schedule that insofar as possible accommodates the needs of each building.

   3.04 Identifies and diagnoses problems in individual and group performance skills, and prescribes appropriate and effective corrective feedback.

   3.05 Designs or selects and uses planned sequences of instruction for the development of instrumental technique and music reading so that students acquire prerequisite skills for the succeeding middle school level of instruction.

   3.06 Teaches to and assesses specified MENC National Standards for Music.

   3.07 Maintains and submits upon request accurate records on enrollment, attendance, and instrumentation.

   3.08 Demonstrates correct techniques for assembly, care, and maintenance of student instruments.

   3.09 Ensures that music and equipment are properly used, maintained, and stored, and that inventory records are accurate and current.

   3.10 Selects and requisitions required music, instructional materials, and supplies.

   3.11 Communicates with parents when students do not (a) attend class regularly, (b) make satisfactory progress, or (c) have their instruments in good playing condition.

3.12 Participates cooperatively in elementary festivals and other designated school and districtwide activities.

Additional responsibilities:

3.13

3.14

4. Minimum qualifications:

  4.01 Teaching license valid for assignment.

  4.02 Working knowledge of band or orchestral string instruments.

  4.03 Perform on own instrument to illustrate and demonstrate correct technique and corrective measures.

  4.04 Strong personal musicianship.

  Additional qualifications:

  4.05

  4.06

  4.07

5. Minimum term of employment: Teacher contract.

6. Salary level: Placement on teacher salary schedule.

7. Evaluation: Performance of this job will be evaluated in accordance with the board's policy on evaluation of professional personnel.

Approved by: _____ Date _____
                          (supervisor)

Received by: _____ Date _____
                          (staff member)

Job Description: Teacher

Teacher

Job Goal: To lead students toward the fulfillment of their potential for intellectual, emotional, physical, and social growth.

Reports to: Building principal or designated administrator.

Performance Requirements:

1. Prepare and present instructional programs appropriate to the student, grade level, and subject assigned, and in keeping with the school district's approved course of study.
2. Assess the progress of students on a regular basis and provide progress reports as required.
3. Maintain a classroom environment that is conducive to learning.
4. Promote and maintain a safe and healthful environment in the classroom and building.
5. Assist the administration in implementing policies and rules governing student life and conduct.
6. Maintain a current file of lesson plans, responsibilities, and procedures for substitute teachers' use.
7. Plan and supervise assignments for teacher aides, volunteers, and student teachers.
8. Establish and maintain effective communication with parents, including reporting on their child's academic progress.
9. Participate in faculty meetings, in-service sessions, and other required building and district meetings.
10. Participate cooperatively in the development and implementation of the district's goals, objectives, and curriculum.
11. Attend and assist when necessary with school events such as musical programs, athletic events, open house, and graduation.
12. Adhere to and support board policies, administrative procedures, and school rules and regulations.
13. Maintain accurate, complete, and current records as required by law, district policy, and administrative regulations.
14. Establish standards of student conduct and administer them in a fair, equitable, and consistent manner.

15. Ensure that all school properties, including materials and equipment, are properly used and maintained.
16. Maintain appropriate work habits, including regular and punctual attendance, and appropriate use of conference and planning time.
17. Respect the confidentiality of records and information regarding students, parents, and teachers in accordance with accepted professional ethics, and state and federal laws.
18. Continue professional growth through attendance at workshops, seminars, conferences, and other in-service activities.
19. Perform other duties as assigned by the building principal or other administrative staff.

Approved by: _____ Date _____
                              (supervisor)

Received by: _____ Date _____
                              (staff member)

As mentioned previously, many districts have only one job description titled "teacher" (see the preceding job description). Because such a job description applies to all teachers, the items included are of necessity nonspecific with respect to subjects taught. Many districts, in fact, combine standards and job descriptions into one document. Such documents are useful to a point, but they do not provide sufficient specificity to help the supervisor do a thorough and professional job of evaluating.

The supervisor, however, can often transform a single job description into a useful document by writing performance indicators for selected items. Such performance indicators would not appear on the job description (unless permission from district officials is received), but would serve as a guide to the supervisor in defining what is meant by selected generic items on the job description.

Many of the items appearing on the music job descriptions may be used as performance indicators on a single (generic) job description. For example, for the first item under the generic teacher job description—"Prepare and present instructional programs appropriate to the student, grade level, and subject assigned, and in keeping with the school district's approved course of study"—the following items taken from the high school band teacher job description could be used as indicators. In the same way, indicators could be written for other items:

1. Conducts rehearsals and performances, demonstrating understanding of differences in style among various types of music.
2. Presents performances of high musical quality in which groups are well disciplined and make a good appearance.
3. Uses music of high quality in a variety of types and styles.
4. Teaches to and assesses specified MENC National Standards for Music.
5. Identifies and diagnoses problems in individual and group performance skills, and prescribes appropriate and effective corrective feedback.
6. Designs or selects and uses planned sequences of instruction for the development of vocal or instrumental technique and music reading.

Endnotes

Baxter, S. G., & Stauffer, S. L. (1988). Music teaching: A review of common practice. In C. Fowler (Ed.), *The Crane Symposium: Toward an understanding of teaching and learning of music performance* (pp. 49–61). Potsdam: Potsdam College of the State University of New York.

Berliner, D. C. (1980). Using research on teaching for the improvement of classroom practice. *Theory Into Practice* 19: 302–308.

Brophy, J. E., & Evertson, C. M. (1976). *Learning from teaching: A developmental perspective.* Boston: Allyn and Bacon.

Duke, R. A. (1999/2000). Measures of instructional effectiveness in music research. *Bulletin of the Council for Research in Music Education* 143: 1–48.

Fisher, C. W., Berliner, D. C., Filby, N. N., Marliane, R., Cahen, L. S., Dishaw, M. M., & Moore, J. E. (1978). *Beginning teacher evaluation study: Phase III-B: A summary of the final report.* San Francisco: State Commission for Teacher Preparation and Licensing.

Grant, J. W., and Drafall, L. E. (1991). Teacher effectiveness research: A review and comparison. *Bulletin of the Council for Research in Music Education* 108: 31–48.

Medley, D. M. (1979). The effectiveness of teachers. In P. L. Peterson & H. J. Walberg (Eds.), *Research on teaching: Concepts, findings, and implications* (pp. 11–27). Berkeley, CA: McCutchan.

National Board for Professional Teaching Standards. (1994). *What teachers should know and be able to do.* Detroit, MI: Author.

Price, H. E. (1983). The effect of conductor academic task presentation, conductor reinforcement, and ensemble practice on performers' musical achievement, attentiveness, and attitude. *Journal of Research in Music Education* 31: 245–258.

Rosenshine, B. V. (1979). Content, time, and direct instruction. In P. L. Peterson & H. J. Walberg (Eds.), *Research on teaching: Concepts, findings, and implications* (pp. 28–56). Berkeley, CA: McCutchan.

Sang, R. C. (1982). *Modified path analysis of a skills-based instructional effectiveness model for beginning teachers in instrumental music education.* Unpublished doctoral dissertation, University of Michigan, Ann Arbor.

Sang, R. C. (1987). A study of the relationship between instrumental music teachers' modeling skills and pupil performance behaviors. *Bulletin of the Council for Research in Music Education* 91: 155–159.

II

The Evaluation Process

I. General Considerations

TEACHER EVALUATION IS A complex process, shaped by different purposes and considerations. The Joint Committee on Standards for Educational Evaluation (1988) lists the following purposes for evaluation:

1. To evaluate entry-level educators before certifying or licensing them to teach.
2. To guide hiring decisions.
3. To identify promising job candidates and assess their qualifications to carry out particular assignments.
4. To guide promotion and tenure decisions.
5. To provide meaningful staff development activities.
6. To recognize and reward meritorious contributions.
7. To identify strengths and where improvement is needed.
8. To prescribe remediation efforts, and, when these fail,
9. To develop fair, valid, and effective cases for termination. (pp. 5–6)

Along with these multiple uses, supervisors must keep several problems associated with the evaluation process in mind. The first is that the process must serve two different purposes: it must help teachers improve instruction and must help administrators make decisions on retention and tenure. The former is referred to as "formative evaluation," while the latter is known as "summative evaluation." A practical evaluation process should help administrators achieve both purposes.

A second and related problem is that supervisors must be supportive and nurturing while at the same time making judgments that could affect a teacher's future. There is really no way out of this fix: a supervisor must do both. The position of the supervisor is much the same, as McNergney and Medley (1984) point out, as that of the teacher who takes responsibility for student growth and learning but who must also exercise judgment through assigning a grade. The evaluation process, then, should be one in which teachers can be helped to improve and can at the same time be held accountable for satisfactory performance.

A third complication is that teacher performance varies. A supervisor must work with three dissimilar types of teachers in different ways:

Type 1—Exemplary teachers. These teachers are usually working on self-identified personal goals to satisfy their own growth needs.

Type 2—Teachers who are competent but have normal growth needs and no serious deficiencies.

Type 3—Teachers with serious deficiencies that require a plan of assistance. If these teachers are not successful in fulfilling the plan, they may be dismissed.

Other concerns related to evaluating teachers of music performance groups have to do with the subject itself. Each subject in the curriculum requires that evaluators have sufficient expertise in the area to generate, interpret, and use the kinds of data peculiar to the discipline. Music is no exception. Music teachers, for their part, are among a minority of teachers who teach elective subjects. They are required, therefore, to accept the responsibility of building high-quality programs by attracting and holding students who enroll by choice. Not all teachers are willing or able to do this.

The key to an evaluation system that can accommodate these diverse purposes and considerations is that it be based on improving instruction rather than designed just to obtain information for retention and tenure. Weber (1987) describes such an approach as focusing on teacher growth and improvement but providing special attention to accountability issues as they affect marginal teachers. The standards and job descriptions presented earlier serve as the basis for a system intended to accommodate the two purposes for evaluation, as well as for working with teachers of varying levels of performance.

II. The Goal-setting Conference

The purpose of the goal-setting conference is to determine the teacher's individual performance goals for the year. Most teachers have three or four such goals. The goal-setting conference should be scheduled according to the timelines of the evaluation calendar. In most districts, this conference is held during the first few weeks of the school year. Some districts prefer to set annual performance goals for the coming school year immediately after the final evaluation in the spring, as shown on the sample Evaluation Calendar (table 1.1). This practice has several advantages: In the first place, the evaluation for the current year is still fresh in the minds of the teacher and the supervisor. Second, the goals will be in place at the beginning of the next school year instead of several weeks later. Finally, the teacher has the summer to think about the goals for the coming school year. From a practical standpoint, however, most music teachers and supervisors are so busy in the late spring that one of the last things on their minds is next year's goals. Because of this, most performance goals are written in the fall during the first few weeks of school.

Characteristics of Goals

The most important characteristic of individual performance goals is that they truly reflect the critical aspects of the job. It is easy to fall into the trap of agreeing to goals that are trivial, chosen because they are easy to accomplish, or are unrelated to the skills required to be an effective teacher of music performance groups. When the observation is completed and analyzed, what the supervisor needs to know is not whether a few goals are being met, but whether the job is being done. Consequently, it is important that the goals be directly related to the skills required for effectiveness in the classroom.

It is also important that long-range considerations that really matter are reflected in the goals, including such things as attracting and

holding students and developing solid individual and group performance and reading skills. The best guarantee of this is that the goals
spring from well-constructed standards and job descriptions. If these
documents are of high quality, the appropriateness and substance of
the goals will be ensured.

Sources of Goals

If the supervisor and teacher reflect on the various sources of goals
before the goal-setting conference, they will usually be able to arrive at
goals that are more appropriate and of higher quality than would other-
wise occur. Sources of goals may be categorized as follows:

Job Descriptions and Standards

These documents serve as the primary source for annual performance
goals. Goals should continue to be drawn from them until the teacher's
performance is satisfactory on all of the items listed. For example, if a
choir sings with a weak, breathy, out-of-tune sound, the supervisor
would want to have one performance goal address this problem. Such a
goal might be that the teacher will "provide effective instructional feedback to the group, leading to improved quality of sound and intonation."

MENC National Standards for Music

These standards specify what each student in America should know
and be able to do in music, and suggest the levels of proficiency that
should be expected. The standards, along with strategies and benchmarks to assess them, have become the basis for most state and local
music instructional standards, and provide a common foundation for
music curricula throughout the nation. They serve as an excellent source
for a teacher's annual individual performance goals (Lehman 1994):

Music Content Standards for Grades K–12

1. Singing, alone and with others, a varied repertoire of music.
2. Performing on instruments, alone and with others, a varied repertoire
   of music.

3. Improvising melodies, variations, and accompaniments.
4. Composing and arranging music within specified guidelines.
5. Reading and notating music.
6. Listening to, analyzing, and describing music.
7. Evaluating music and music performances.
8. Understanding relationships between music, the other arts, and disciplines outside the arts.
9. Understanding music in relation to history and culture. (Lehman 1994, p. vi)

For resources on the MENC Standards, see Appendix H.

The Previous Year's Evaluation

This document should always be reviewed as a source for goals. The final evaluation form invariably has a section where deficiencies needing improvement are listed. Anything appearing in this category should be noted and carried over as a performance goal for the following year.

The Curriculum

Almost all districts have a written scope and sequence or a curriculum guide of some kind that teachers are expected to follow. This document is a good source for individual performance goals, especially in cases where particular facets of the instructional program need strengthening or are not being addressed.

Program Evaluation

This entails the assessment of all aspects of a districtwide music education program. MENC (the National Association for Music Education) specifies that program evaluation should provide data on student achievement, scheduling, course offerings, staffing, materials and equipment, and facilities, so that teachers and administrators have a solid basis for making decisions (George et al. 1986). Program evaluation should be based on clear objectives, and data on these objectives may be gathered in any way that seems fitting, including observation of students, checklists, published and teacher-made tests, and other teacher or supervisor-based procedures.

The relationship between teacher evaluation and program evaluation is not always clear. Effective program evaluation reveals strengths and weaknesses in the program that have implications for teacher evaluation and that may serve as a source for teacher goals. But data from program evaluation must be used with extreme care in teacher evaluation. Teachers cannot and should not be held responsible for things that often make their jobs impossible, such as faulty schedules, inadequate equipment or facilities, staffing problems, poor teaching of prerequisite skills, and low enrollment in feeder schools.

A case in point is the 2001 educational law No Child Left Behind. This program, with its emphasis on rigorous national and state testing in math and reading, has caused many school districts to cut back or eliminate elective courses such as music. So-called pull-out programs—where students are taken out of class for band, orchestra, or choir—have been especially hard hit. It is up to the administration to contend with these problems. Instances occur, however, in which program weaknesses can be attributed to teacher performance. It is in these cases that program evaluation serves as a source for teacher performance goals.

Information Supplied by the Teacher

It is often productive during the conference to discuss with the teacher aspects of the program that may lead to goals. Sometimes the teacher should bring pertinent information in writing to the conference. For example, he or she might bring data from the following list of topics:

1. The sequence of instruction for developing individual technique
2. The sequence of instruction for teaching music reading
3. Individual student progress assessment and monitoring procedures
4. Results of student assessments on MENC standards
5. Inventory records
6. Enrollment records
7. Instrumentation records
8. How voices are selected and placed
9. The teacher's grading system
10. Recruiting calendar and activities

Annual or Special Goals of the District, School, or Music Program

The district, an individual school, or the districtwide music program may elect to focus on a particular goal or goals for a school year. Such goals may address, for example, improved classroom management, instrumental or vocal technique, or parent and citizen involvement in the instructional program. These special goals should always be reviewed, and where germane they should be reflected in the teacher's individual performance goals for the year.

Districtwide Tests

Districtwide tests, administered on an annual basis, are a good source for goals. For example, some districts test students on their ability to read music. Where the results indicate that students are not doing satisfactorily, a performance goal may be written specifying the supervisor's expectations.

Goals selected for the year will vary according to the teacher. During hiring interviews, supervisors can ask beginning teachers and experienced teachers who are new to the district to review job descriptions and standards to identify their own strengths and areas where further personal growth is needed. This self-assessment can serve as a source for personal performance goals for the coming school year. Supervisors should also observe any teachers who are new to the district once or twice for at least part of a class period before the goal-setting conference. In this way the supervisor will have a better idea of the kinds of goals that will be most appropriate for each teacher.

In the same way that performance goals vary according to teachers, the supervisor's role in determining those goals will differ. For teachers who are new to the district, the supervisor will normally take the lead in the goal-setting process. If the teacher is to have four goals for the year, the supervisor will want to specify at least two and base these on the standards and job descriptions. The teacher and supervisor should then mutually agree on the remaining goals, taking into consideration the teacher's expressed interests and needs.

For teachers whose performance is a matter for concern, supervisors typically specify all of the performance goals. Depending on the degree of concern, supervisors would still be well advised to consider asking the teacher to choose one goal.

There are always those teachers who do exemplary work year after year and whose performance elicits no concerns. It is usually best to let such teachers take the lead in setting goals, as they know their own strengths and interests and can select goals for their own personal growth better than anyone.

A sample form for writing individual performance goals is given in Appendix A. Note that each goal is written on a form of its own. For example, if a teacher has three goals, three forms would be required. (When designing forms for local use, provide more space for writing than is shown in the examples.)

III. The Pre-observation Conference

The pre-observation conference is one of the most important components of the evaluation cycle. Both the teacher and the supervisor should leave this meeting with a clear understanding of the following:

1. The type of class and activities that will be observed. In most cases this will be a typical rehearsal
2. What has been going on in rehearsals up to the point of the observation
3. The instructional objectives for this particular class
4. How the supervisor will be collecting data during the observation
5. Each of these items should be thoroughly discussed and put into writing on an appropriate form (see Appendix B) so that misunderstandings are avoided

In preparing for the pre-observation conference, the supervisor may wish to ask the teacher to submit, in advance, documents that the supervisor may need as background. This same information is useful for the goal-setting conference, and may include, among other things, data on enrollment, instrumentation, inventory, and instructional sequences for teaching technique or reading (see "Sources of Goals" earlier in this section for additional items). Such background materials often provide clues about strengths and weaknesses in the program and become a possible source for goals and objectives.

The climate the supervisor should try to create for the pre-observation conference is that of a shared sense of responsibility. This will vary, of course, with the status of the teacher. Just as is the case in the goal-setting process, the supervisor will exercise more control with new teachers or with teachers who have serious deficiencies. Teachers who are performing in a satisfactory manner with normal growth needs and no serious deficiencies should share the responsibilities for the conference with the supervisor. Exemplary teachers may well take the lead in determining objectives for the observation as well as in specifying the types of data collection that would serve them best.

One of the first subjects taken up at the conference should be the type of class to be observed. In music performance classes, the normal setting for instruction is the rehearsal. Consequently, a supervisor needs to know several things: What will be the general plan of the rehearsal? Will there be a warm-up period, a time for working on group technique, or a time for teaching music reading? What materials will be used? What pieces will be played or sung? It is particularly important to know the stage of preparation of the various pieces, as there is a big difference between how the supervisor analyzes instruction a few days before a concert when pieces should be being polished and how he or she makes the same analysis a few days after a concert when new music has been distributed and students are still learning the notes.

Selection of Goals and Objectives

Distinguishing Between Goals and Objectives

The term "goal" is usually used for long-range instructional aims. Examples include the general goals of a school district, the goals of a total music program, or the annual performance goals of individual teachers. The term "objective" is usually used for aims of a shorter range, such as those for a unit of instruction or a daily lesson. "Objectives" will be used here for those instructional aims that come out of the pre-observation conference and are intended to be accomplished during the observation itself.

Characteristics of Objectives

Objectives, like goals, must be of substance and must truly reflect the most important aspects of the job. They must also be written in a way that is consistent with how teachers really operate. Objectives that focus on narrow behaviors, such as "given three attempts to play a designated passage at a prescribed tempo, the ensemble will perform the passage with 80% accuracy," often satisfy textbook or administrative requirements, but they contribute little to the evaluation process.

When selecting objectives to be used in observing instruction, supervisors must recognize that most teachers do not use predetermined objectives as the basis for planning instruction. Instead, they focus on the type of learning activities they want to provide for students and weigh things such as content and materials; their own interests, skills, and limitations; the needs of students; and long-range goals. This claim is substantiated by more than one researcher (Shavelson & Stern 1981; Taylor 1970; Zahorik 1975), and most experienced observers would agree that these findings are consistent with how teachers of performance groups really plan instruction.

In long-range terms, the repertoire, rather than a set of predetermined objectives, becomes the focus of planning for instruction and is selected according to the teacher's interests or the ensemble's strengths and weaknesses. In short-range terms, the starting point for organizing a rehearsal is usually a flow of activities, such as a warm-up period, a time for working on group technique, and a time for working on repertoire. In elementary band or orchestra, the organizing focus for most teachers—once position, breathing, and tone production are established—is the method book, not objectives. This may not be the approach advocated by textbooks and theorists, but it is almost always the case in music performance classes.

Indeed, one must always consider the total context of instruction when selecting objectives to be used in observations. Objectives considered apart from context are not likely to fit into the flow of activities, forcing the teacher to function in an unnatural way. When selected with the flow of instruction in mind, objectives are easily addressed through either the warm-up, technique, or repertory portions of the rehearsal, or through a combination of these activities.

One simple and practical way to select objectives consistent with how teachers operate is to have the teacher state what he or she intends to work on during the warm-up and technique portions of the class and on each piece to be rehearsed. These statements can then be translated into objectives. If, for example, a teacher intends to clear up problems in balance or ensemble cohesiveness in a particular section of a piece, that intention could be written out as an objective. Such an objective would be consistent with how the teacher works when the supervisor is not in the room, and helps to avoid the artificiality of having to teach to textbook-style objectives written for observation days only.

Objectives selected for observation must also be chosen so that they are achievable, or at least so progress can be shown during a single period of instruction. This is not to say that long-range instructional aims that must continually be addressed should be avoided. Tone quality and intonation, for example, cannot be achieved in one rehearsal without ever having to be taught again. It is better to select objectives in these areas that are directed to the kind of improvement that can be realized during a single period of instruction.

A final consideration concerning the characteristics of objectives is related to the phenomenon known as "teaching to an objective." Supervisors who use this approach have been known to downgrade the performance of teachers who deviate in any way from prescribed objectives. Supervisors must remember that teachers of performance groups seldom teach to one objective at a time. Many interrelated problems, such as tone quality, intonation, part accuracy, style, and the like, are being addressed simultaneously, and unexpected things that must be addressed often come up in rehearsals. It is, in fact, often more important to fix these things than to complete what one set out to do in the first place.

Two considerations, therefore, must be kept in mind if supervisors are going to insist that teachers teach to an objective. First, teachers must be allowed the flexibility to adjust the lesson, if, in their judgment, more effective instruction will result. Second (and this is the key to the problem of teaching to an objective), the objective must be written in a way that fits naturally into the flow of instruction. In this way, the teacher can teach without fear of being caught off-task. The problem is not so much insisting that the teacher teach to an objective as it is writing good objectives that are consistent with a teacher's normal rehearsal procedures. When this is done, the teacher in most cases will be teaching naturally to an objective, and the supervisor can concentrate on the quality of instruction.

Reporting the Results of the Pre-observation Conference

When the supervisor and teacher have agreed on the objectives, those objectives should be written on a form similar to the sample in Appendix B. The objectives should be written in the space provided under "Objective(s) of the lesson." When the remaining categories on the form have been completed, expectations for the observation will be well defined. Examples of the type of objectives that fit into normal rehearsal procedures follow (the focus of each can be narrowed if desired):

1. Rehearse specified sections of pieces under preparation, diagnosing problems and prescribing corrective procedures resulting in improved performance. (A narrower focus might be to achieve balance or part accuracy.)
2. Improve the tone quality of the choir through modeling and giving instructional feedback to help the students develop frontal resonance.
3. Teach music reading during a portion of the rehearsal, using techniques and methods belonging to a carefully sequenced and comprehensive approach to the subject. (A narrower focus might be to teach specific rhythms.)
4. Teach lessons to beginning band or orchestra students before introducing a method book, using a step-by-step approach to the fundamentals of breathing, playing position, embouchure, and music reading.
5. In a selected piece (e.g., a theme and variations or a Bach fugue), identify and explain the compositional devices and techniques used to provide unity and variety and tension and release (Lehman 1996, p. 112).
6. Ensure that students enter the room in an orderly manner and do not distract the teacher or other students during the rehearsal.

The pre-observation form has space for listing how data will be recorded by the supervisor (see Item V in Appendix B). The recording techniques chosen should be appropriate to the kind of information sought; in this case, they should be chosen from among techniques that are particularly useful in evaluating music performance classes.

IV. The Observation

Classroom observation is not easy. It involves much more than walking into the room with a checklist and a pencil. The skills and knowledge necessary to be an effective observer are acquired only through experience, practice, and study.

First of all, supervisors need a strong background in music. Then they need to develop a framework of some kind through which to look at instruction in order to make sense of what is going on in the classroom. Supervisors also need a strong background in teaching methods, curriculum, materials, and psychology of learning. They must be able to use a variety of techniques for recording information, ranging from the descriptive to the judgmental and from those dealing with selective behaviors to the all-encompassing. In addition to all of this, supervisors must be alert and keenly perceptive, having what Kounin (1970) calls "withitness," which he defines as the ability to see continuously everything that is going on in the classroom.

Supervisors must also be aware that their presence changes the climate in the classroom. Teachers are likely to be uncomfortable, especially when there are questions of retention, dismissal, or tenure, or when their "comfort zone"—that personal level of performance with which a teacher becomes satisfied and stops striving to improve—has been invaded.

Students are also affected by the novelty of a supervisor's presence. They are often distracted in the same way by video or audio cassette equipment (when that equipment is used to record classroom activities in place of personal observation by the supervisor) unless they have time to get used to it. Students are naturally curious about any changes in normal routines, especially if these include outside individuals. This can change the way they respond in the rehearsal setting, and must be taken into account during observations.

Techniques and Methods for Recording Information

Descriptive Versus Judgmental Techniques

The main task of the supervisor is to make sense of what is going on in the classroom. Some authorities on evaluation insist that observations should be described only in terms of descriptive statements and that anything judgmental or subjective should be avoided during the observation. In fact—because the line between description and judgment is often blurred—it is difficult to restrict recorded statements to those that are strictly descriptive and objective. As Eisner (1979) points out, "Educational criticism relies upon judgment" (p. 18). Unless one has agreed to take only descriptive data for a special focus, it is better not to exclude statements of a subjective nature when they help to describe what is seen and heard.

Assessments about appropriateness and context are best made as they occur. If a supervisor simply describes or counts the instances of certain behaviors, he or she runs the risk of missing something of real importance. The quality of experiences students are having, for example, is often difficult to express in objective or descriptive terms.

Whether or not a supervisor believes in recording only descriptive data, he or she must recognize the difference between what simply describes and what is judgmental. A statement such as "You spent too long on that first piece" is not only judgmental but it is also likely to make the teacher unnecessarily defensive. The same information could be stated in descriptive terms as "Forty minutes of the fifty-minute period were spent on the first piece"—a purely descriptive statement with no judgmental implications.

A good rule to follow is to stick with objective statements when they best describe what is happening. For example, it is better to say, "Several students were not participating" than "The students were not interested." But when statements that describe the quality of events are needed, one should not be reluctant to be subjective. Statements such as "Thirty minutes into the lesson and no instructional feedback of substance has occurred" or "The teacher is trying to raise the sagging pitch of the group by pointing upward when the problem is an unfocused, out-of-tune sound" describe significant classroom events more accurately than purely descriptive language. With these considerations in mind, the supervisor is ready to decide how to record information.

Selective Verbatim

Acheson and Gall (1987) define *selective verbatim* as a technique for recording classroom events in which the supervisor makes a verbatim record of exactly what is said, that is, a verbatim transcript. Not all verbal events are recorded, however. Supervisor and teacher select beforehand certain kinds of verbal events to be written down; in this sense, the verbatim record is intended to be "selective." (p. 81)

Selective verbatim is a recording technique often used for what is known as focused observation, where the recording of information is limited to certain classroom events, and allows teacher and supervisor to isolate and focus on specific areas of interest or concern. Because no attempt is made to record everything that is going on, it is easy for the supervisor to make a verbatim record of the specific area or areas selected for observation. The supervisor simply records in writing all statements by the teacher and the students that are pertinent to the information sought. These can be analyzed later for substance and appropriateness.

One of the areas for which selective verbatim is a particularly useful recording technique is instruction. To determine if the teacher is providing instructional feedback that is appropriate, substantive, and effective, the supervisor records verbatim instructional feedback given to students. This technique can, of course, include all instructional feedback or can be limited to one or two aspects, such as tone quality or intonation.

Quality of interaction in the classroom is another area for which useful information can be obtained through selective verbatim. In this case the teacher and supervisor are interested in positive and negative aspects of interaction with students, including the general emotional tone of the classroom. A simple technique is to record all instances of positive and negative reinforcement by the teacher. Another approach is to record all comments of both teacher and students that reflect some kind of emotional tone, such as frustration or hostility.

Selective verbatim is also useful in obtaining information on aspects of classroom management. When management problems are severe, the supervisor is taxed to record all pertinent data, even though recording efforts are limited to this one dimension of the teacher's responsibilities.

At-task

One of the findings of teacher effectiveness research is that the more time students spend actively engaged in learning tasks, the more they learn (Rosenshine 1979). Because of this, teachers and supervisors need information on the active participation of students in rehearsals. Instruments have been developed through which detailed information on at-task behavior of individual students can be recorded (Acheson & Gall 1987). Such instruments are especially useful in classes where a variety of learning activities occur. In music performance classes, however, where all students are usually engaged in a common task, little sophistication is required to record off-task behavior.

Verbal Flow

Verbal flow, as a recording technique for performing groups, is something of a misnomer. In the rehearsal setting, most of the talking is done by the teacher. It is, nevertheless, important to know something about where verbal instruction is being directed. For example, teachers often have a tendency to talk to students in the front of the group at the expense of those to the sides or rear. At other times, most instruction may be directed at the sections the teacher knows best or to individuals who are favored—or not favored—by the teacher. Recording of verbal flow reveals these tendencies and patterns, and thus provides information helpful in improving instruction.

Video and Audio Recording

Almost all schools now have equipment for video and audio recording. These techniques are among the most useful for obtaining information on classroom performance; at the same time, they often raise the anxiety level of teachers. For this reason it is a good idea in most cases for teachers to view or hear the tape alone and keep it in their possession.

After viewing or hearing a tape alone, teachers usually become aware of things needing improvement and are willing to discuss these with the supervisor. It is also productive for teacher and supervisor to view or hear the tape together, after the teacher has seen or heard it alone. In this way both are able to ask questions and to discuss how a lesson went. This approach also makes it possible for the supervisor to learn the thinking behind the teacher's instructional decisions.

Video and audio recording can be used with both focused and comprehensive observations. For example, the supervisor can use an audio recording to make sure everything has been entered correctly on a selective verbatim. When doing a comprehensive observation, the supervisor can use either audio or video recordings for review or to gain additional information. (For a thorough description of various observation techniques, see Acheson and Gall 1987, 1997).

Comprehensive Observation

One technique that is often overlooked in discussions of various ways to record information is that of comprehensive observation. This entails simply going into the classroom with no preconceptions and recording everything essential about the teacher's performance as it occurs. Unlike focused observation, which is limited to recording information on specified classroom events or areas of instruction, comprehensive observation can provide a true picture of a teacher's overall performance.

While comprehensive observation can be used with any teacher, it is especially appropriate for use with beginning teachers or experienced teachers who are new to the district. In these cases, the supervisor is able to determine the teacher's level of performance and gains a sufficient background of information to provide direction for future objectives and evaluation activities. The comprehensive approach is likewise effective when trying to identify deficiencies for a teacher whose performance is not satisfactory.

Comprehensive observation can also be useful in connection with what is known in some districts as the review of services. Such a review is sometimes used when the performance of a teacher is seriously called into question.

Although used infrequently, the Salt Lake City schools have since 1974

allowed parents, students, principals, or even other teachers to request a "review of services" when they have a complaint about a teacher. If an impartial review panel determines that the accusations are serious and valid, the teacher can be placed on a five-month "remediation review." Four people work with him [or her] to correct the problem: the principal, a learning specialist, and two colleagues, one of whom helps protect the teacher's due-process rights. (Williams et al. 1981)

Most problems in teacher performance, however, are resolved in other ways before getting to the review of services stage. (The Salt Lake City

"Review of Services" was still in effect, as confirmed by a telephone conversation in December 2005.)

Checklists

Checklists are commonly used by many observers to obtain information during comprehensive classroom observations. The designers of some checklists choose the behaviors to be evaluated from research; on other lists, the behaviors are simply those that the list maker believes to be the characteristics of effective teachers. The observer makes a mark on the list in the space provided as each behavior occurs. The number of items on such lists can range into the hundreds.

The main problem with checklists is that they cannot adequately describe everything going on in a classroom. All that a checklist tells the observer is whether certain behaviors or events occurred, and even these notations are limited to what is on the checklist. Speaking of his uneasiness with conventional methods of evaluation, Eisner (1979) draws an analogy that could be applied to the limitations of checklists:

> To cast a net into the sea that is unintentionally designed to let most of the fish get away, and then to conclude from those that are caught of what the variety of fish in the sea consists is, at the very least, a sampling error of the first order. Then to describe the fish that are caught in terms of their length and weight is to reduce radically what we can know about the qualitative features of the ones that have been caught, not to mention the features of those that the net failed to catch in the first place. (p. 14)

Eisner cites as further deficiencies of checklists their inability to account for context and quality. Because of these shortcomings, checklists give us an inaccurate and unrealistic picture of what is really happening in the classroom, and we are likely to misinterpret the information we do get from them. To illustrate the problem of context, an evaluator observing a music performance class two days before a concert would expect most teacher interventions to be in the direction of polishing and putting the final touches on the performance. What is one to think if the group is still struggling for the right notes? This would be perfectly appropriate two days after a concert, when new and unfamiliar music is being rehearsed. But checklists make no provision for such a consideration of context.

Neither do checklists make provision for recording the quality of instruction. An observer, for example, may make an impressive number of checks after the behavior "provides corrective feedback." Completely ignored is the fact that the feedback may be based on faulty diagnosis or prescription, making it inappropriate or even counterproductive.

Additional inadequacies of checklists have been identified by Griffith (1975), who notes that checklists usually deal with details, often superficial, rather than with broad and fundamental issues. Checklists contain many items of varying significance, rarely with any attempt to weigh their relative importance. Because checklists are impersonal, they can induce supervisors to make superficial judgments without patient reflection and careful analysis.

The Observation Guide

Most observers find some kind of observation instrument useful in helping to describe what is seen and heard in the classroom. Because of the well-documented inadequacies of checklists, another type of instrument is needed. Such an instrument needs to help the observer avoid missing important events occurring in the classroom and must help the observer make sense of classroom activity.

The observation guide is such an instrument. It is not a checklist in that the observer does not merely check off or tally instances of behaviors. Rather, it is scanned several times during an observation to ensure that events of importance are not being missed. It is actually a kind of "trigger list," reminding the observer of things to look for, and helping to generate useful information. A helpful guide goes beyond superficial and easily observable aspects of teaching and learning, and its use requires skill and judgment on the part of the supervisor. It should not be considered all-inclusive or static, but should grow and change with the observer.

Observation guides, like standards and job descriptions, should be based on familiarity with the findings of teacher effectiveness research. A good way to develop an observation guide is to establish a broad framework by selecting several main categories and listing appropriate items under each category. There is no hard-and-fast rule for determining the number and titles of the categories.

The sample Observation Guide (in Appendix C) includes a group of learning outcomes in addition to those that are related to individual and group skill development. The items have to do with helping students learn something about the music they are performing through applying knowledge of musical structure and historical considerations to the repertoire. The list could easily go beyond this into areas such as aesthetic judgment and multicultural awareness if desired. Instruction in most performance groups, however, is usually limited—rightly or wrongly—to the development of individual and group performance skills. Whether a teacher should be evaluated on any other basis should be determined by an individual school district's expectations as given in program goals, curriculum documents, and job descriptions.

Procedures for Recording Information

With the objectives for the lesson in hand, and with the method of collecting data determined, the supervisor is ready to begin recording information. A good way to proceed is to write a heading for each major section of the rehearsal as it occurs and to record information under those headings as the rehearsal unfolds. The first heading may well be "Getting Started," followed by "Warm-up" and then "Repertoire," with the individual pieces taught listed underneath. Additional headings may be used if the rehearsal has other major sections, such as the teaching of technique or music reading.

Remarks should be recorded as events occur (or do not occur). This is relatively easy to do if selective verbatim, verbal flow, or at-task techniques are being used, but comprehensive observation is more challenging. It is impossible, and probably not even desirable, to get a written record of everything that is said or done in the classroom. An observer cannot and should not try to record everything. A rehearsal includes many rapidly changing, complex events. The observer needs to screen out those events that do not apply and focus on those that are essential. Because so many things are happening so fast, it is helpful for observers to use abbreviations of their own making. Instructional feedback, for example, becomes "IF," and positive reinforcement becomes "PR." Each observer may develop other simple abbreviations.

On completion of the observation, the supervisor is ready to return to the office to analyze and interpret the information and to prepare for the post-observation conference with the teacher.

V. Analyzing Instruction

It has been said that good teaching is easy to recognize but hard to define. The complexity of teaching behavior is what makes this statement true. Brophy and Evertson (1976) have characterized this complexity as follows:

Effective teaching is not simply a matter of implementing a small number of basic teaching skills. Instead, effective teaching requires the ability to implement a very large number of diagnostic, instructional, managerial, and therapeutic skills, tailoring behavior in specific contexts and situations to the specific needs of the moment. Effective teachers must not only be able to do a large number of things; they also must be able to recognize which of the many things they know how to do applies to a given moment and be able to follow through by performing the behavior effectively. (p. 159)

The complexity of the teaching process is, in part, what makes the task of analyzing instruction so demanding. The supervisor needs to discover patterns of teacher behavior, to know which of these patterns are important, and to find any relationships that may exist between and among such patterns in order to unravel the meaning of what is seen and heard (McNergney & Medley 1984). A useful first step in analyzing instruction is to assess the performance level of the band, choir, or orchestra.

Characteristics of Music Groups

A performance-level assessment based on general characteristics of a group's performance yields the first clues regarding the teacher's effectiveness and gives the supervisor a sense of the quality of instruction that is taking place. For such an assessment, performance groups may be categorized as follows:

1. The group just plows through pieces with little or no instructional feedback of substance. This is the case with many instrumental and choral groups. The lack of substantial instructional feedback is reflected in the poor-to-mediocre quality of these groups.

2. The group plays or sings with good technique. Students are learning solid individual and group skills, and fundamentals are well
   taught. Abundant instructional feedback of substance and appropriateness is provided. Much effective instruction goes on in
   groups of this type, and they play or sing well from a technical
   standpoint. They lack, however, the musical and expressive quali-
   ties of truly fine ensembles.
3. The group's performance has an artistic and expressive dimension.
   This characterizes the finest ensembles. Solid technical skills are a
   prerequisite for this category.
4. The students in the group know something about the music they
   are playing. They have knowledge beyond the technical and expressive abilities and skills required to perform well. Even groups
   whose performance level is exemplary are seldom strong on this
   characteristic.

Music reading is a related issue. A "plow-through" group rarely reads
well. A group that has well-developed technique may or may not possess
strong reading skills. Teachers must develop their students' reading skills
if the students are to achieve musical independence.

A group showing the last three characteristics (technique, artistry, and
knowledge) would be truly exemplary in every respect. A group with only
strong technical skills would be very good, but still have room to improve.
A supervisor can, through informal observation or hearing a group in
concert, gain a good general impression of its ability level. This is a first
step in the analysis of instruction, and provides a good background for
information recorded during formal observations of rehearsals.

Whether to include instruction on history, theory, and form in the rehearsal has been a continuing professional issue for many years, calling
into question our deepest beliefs about music education. While some
writers exhort teachers to go beyond performance, most teachers continue to use what Baxter and Stauffer (1988) refer to as "common practice": teaching as they have been taught, as they see others teach, and
using "what works" based upon their own experience. One must also
keep practical considerations in mind. Cutietta (1986) cites the following as reasons that militate against going "beyond performance" in the
ensemble rehearsal: the attitude that students join performance classes
expecting to perform and that learning activities should be in line with

student goals and expectations; the fact that the rehearsal setting (seating, instruments, stands) does not lend itself easily to teaching skills other than those of performance; and the practical matter of class size, which is usually too large for effective presentation of academic subjects.

Even so, a good case can be made for a minimum set of essential learnings (see Appendixes C and D) that can be taught without seriously inhibiting the flow of the rehearsal. Students performing a band transcription of a piece by Richard Wagner, for example, should grasp the concept of modulation; students performing a fugue should understand how the piece goes together. In exceptional groups, students learn more than skills—they also learn something about the music itself. At the same time, it should be recognized that a secondary school rehearsal setting has its limitations on what can be taught. A big difference exists between such a setting and a college music degree program, where history, theory, and analysis are dealt with in separate courses that often extend for more than one year.

Fortunately, a number of publishers have come out with excellent curriculum materials designed to help in teaching "about the music." The MENC content standards, achievement standards, and assessment strategies provide a common foundation for this aspect of the curriculum. If teaching about the music is part of a district's job descriptions, the supervisor may refer teachers to materials such as those listed in Appendix H (Resources).

The Warm-up

It is common to spend the first part of a rehearsal in what is known as the warm-up. What occurs during the warm-up should be analyzed carefully. In the first place, a good warm-up must have a purpose. It should not be a perfunctory or mechanical playing or singing of familiar scales and exercises without apparent instructional aims. This is not to say that a teacher cannot conduct an effective warm-up with a minimum of materials or exercises. It is the presence of a purpose, not the number of exercises used to achieve that purpose, that is important. Following are some indicators to use in analyzing the warm-up:

1. Is there an apparent purpose?
2. Are the activities consistent with the purpose?

3. Is the warm-up productive?
4. Is a businesslike attitude established for the rehearsal?
5. Are correct posture and position insisted upon?
6. Is tone quality a high priority?
7. Is the pitch center of the group established through careful attention to intonation?
8. Are correct breathing and airflow stressed?
9. In the case of choir, is technique taught as part of the warm-up?
10. Are overblowing and oversinging avoided?

The warm-up period will usually reveal whether the teacher works with priorities in mind. Revelli (n.d.), asking the question "What are the elements that constitute a satisfying music performance?" has generated a list of priorities that apply to both the warm-up and the rehearsal in general:

1. Tone quality (according to Revelli, the most prized possession of a musician)
2. Intonation
3. Rhythm
4. The right note
5. Interpretation

Diagnostic/Prescriptive Instruction

According to the late John Paynter, "a good conductor must be able to hear what is going on, while it is going on, and suggest what to do to change it" (quoted in Neidig 1979, p. 12). This statement admirably characterizes diagnostic/prescriptive instruction.

The accomplishment of the complex task described by Paynter requires the exhibition of many and varied teaching behaviors. The fact that the director must exhibit so many behaviors generates in turn a great deal of data, all of which the supervisor must consider in trying to find meaning in what is observed. Because of this, the supervisor should have in mind some kind of framework for looking at instruction. Such a framework should help in assigning significance and appropriateness to teaching behaviors, and should help in showing how these behaviors are related. The diagnostic/prescriptive process provides such a framework.

Sound Concept

The basis for effective diagnostic/prescriptive instruction in music performance groups is that the teacher has a clear concept of how an excellent band, choir, or orchestra sounds. The things a teacher does or does not do from an instructional standpoint are largely determined by the quality of this "sound concept," in that he or she will be assessing the group's efforts against this standard held in the mind's ear. If the sound concept is unclear or of mediocre quality, it will be impossible for the teacher to give appropriate and effective instructional feedback; conversely, a sound concept of high quality provides the basis for instruction of high quality. The supervisor must keep this in mind, because problems in teacher performance can often be traced back to an inadequate sound concept. When this is the case, the supervisor must help the teacher acquire a good concept.

How a sound concept of high quality is acquired is not easy to say. Recognizing and appreciating the performance of fine professional and amateur groups is certainly fundamental, but it does not guarantee that the listener will acquire a good sound concept. Being an excellent performer may be part of the answer, but again, this qualification is no guarantee that a teacher will acquire a good ensemble sound concept. One would expect that a teacher's playing in fine groups would ensure the development of a good sound concept, but again, this is no guarantee. In fine groups, it is the director, not the student, who has the responsibility for finding and fixing the problems. Unless a student is unusually disciplined and perceptive, most of what the director is doing goes right on by.

It is also possible to have a good sound concept and still provide inappropriate instructional feedback. In such cases teachers have the concept, but do not use it effectively as a standard against which to assess the efforts of their groups. Some teachers "know what they want but don't know how to get it." Others who do not hear things clearly are perhaps too close to the day-to-day problems of their groups and need to stand back to hear things as they really are. Still others are oblivious or deceiving themselves about what they are hearing. All too familiar is the conductor whose gestures and facial expressions suggest that it is the New York Philharmonic or the RIAS Kammerchor and not his or her own group that is onstage. In all of these cases, the teacher can often be helped. The supervisor needs to be able to differentiate between, and be prepared to deal with, these root causes of ineffective instruction.

Applying Diagnostic/Prescriptive Principles

As the rehearsal unfolds, the supervisor should ask the following questions:

1. *Does the teacher recognize when something is wrong?* This is the first step of the diagnostic/prescriptive process. The teacher who knows something is wrong but cannot identify it at least has a basis for improvement. It is, however, not always easy to tell if a teacher knows something is wrong. Sometimes, for example, because of individual priorities, the teacher chooses not to attend to each error or problem as it occurs. Nonetheless, in most cases, the supervisor can tell that a teacher is not aware that something is wrong when unaddressed deficiencies are pervasive and the group fails to improve, not only during the daily rehearsal but also over a span of weeks or months.

   In order to be sure that the teacher does not know when something is wrong, the supervisor should talk to him or her. Questions such as "Are you satisfied with the sound of your group?" are a good way to open such a conversation, which should reveal whether the teacher is aware of something wrong. If, in the course of the conversation, it becomes evident that the teacher doesn't know, then the supervisor must help the teacher become aware of the deficiencies.

2. *Does the teacher identify the right problems?* This is the key step in the process. Unless the teacher finds the right problems—the right things to fix—he or she will be working on the wrong things during the rehearsal. The real question, as Drucker (1964) points out in another context, "is not how to do things right, but how to find the right things to do, and to concentrate resources and efforts on them" (p. 6).

   The only way, of course, to know whether the teacher is finding the right problems is for the supervisor to know what they are. The competent supervisor is one who, among other things, knows when the teacher is working on the right things.

3. *Does the teacher prescribe the right solution to the problem?* Sometimes the teacher finds the problem but proposes a "solution" that will not fix it. For example, the teacher who attempts to fix intonation when the group has serious problems in tone production should be addressing the problem through improving tone quality

rather than admonishing the group to play or sing higher or lower. As long as tone is uncentered and unfocused, intonation problems will exist. As in the other steps of the process, the supervisor must know when the prescribed solution is appropriate.

4. *Does the teacher persist in solving problems, and if not, does he or she leave the problem by default or by design?* One of the characteristics of a successful rehearsal is that things sound better at the end than they did at the beginning. Instances occur when teachers know a problem exists, identify it accurately, prescribe the right solution, and still do not get results. Many times this is because of a lack of persistence. Still, it is often appropriate to leave a problem unfixed. This is especially true when the teacher senses that the pursuit of the solution is becoming unproductive. In such cases, the teacher leaves the problem by design, with the intent of coming back to it at a better time.

Sometimes, however, teachers leave problems by default rather than by design. Extreme cases of this occur when the teacher merely tells the students the solution or provides little feedback of substance before moving on. When asked why identified problems still exist after weeks or months, it is not uncommon for a teacher to say, "I don't know why they still do it that way—I told them." Truman Hutton, the late supervisor of instrumental music for the Los Angeles School District, used to say "telling is not teaching." Just mentioning corrections and not pursuing them is not enough. The teacher has to persist and take responsibility for getting results, or, if not, leave a problem by design with the intent of returning to it at a more favorable time.

Finally, it should be noted that a teacher can identify problems, prescribe what are apparently correct solutions, persist, and still not get good results. The supervisor needs to keep in mind that teaching is about outcomes to be achieved, not tasks to be performed, and that in teaching the art of music anything short of excellence indicates a need for improvement.

VI. The Post-observation Conference

The post-observation conference is a meeting between teacher and supervisor about the just-completed observation. The conference should be held within a day or two of the observation, allowing time for reflection but soon enough for events to be fresh in the minds of both parties. The setting should be informal. The worst possible setting is the supervisor facing a teacher across a desk. It is much better to sit together at a table in the supervisor's office, or to meet in a conference room.

Planning for the post-observation conference should be done carefully. The supervisor needs to take adequate time to reflect on what was seen and heard, to analyze it, and to describe it in writing so that it is easily understood. How the data are presented may range from a written analysis of the observation (see Appendix D) to descriptive data intended to be discussed and analyzed together. Formal observations using the clinical supervision model usually require a written analysis. Descriptive data intended for collaborative use are sometimes used for informal observations or for exemplary teachers. In any case, the performance level of the teacher will usually be the determining factor as to which approach is used. For beginning teachers, and for those with performance deficiencies, a written analysis based on the information recorded during the observation, along with the supervisor's suggestions for improvement, is preferred.

The written report of the observation should be prepared in time for the teacher to read it before the conference. Enough time should then be set aside for the meeting so that both parties participating can have a thorough discussion of the data. The form needs to be signed by both the teacher and the supervisor. If, after an exchange of views, the report needs to be revised, that can be done, and the teacher can sign it after the revision is complete. The conclusions from the conference, along with those from similar conferences held during the year, will serve as the basis for the final written evaluation at the end of the year.

Finally, supervisors should avoid dominating, as is their tendency, the post-observation conference. Blumberg and Cusick (1970) found that during conferences supervisors gave information about five times as often as they asked for it from teachers, and that they were usually directive in their statements, controlling teachers most of the time. Supervisors must guard against these inclinations so that teachers always have the freedom to express their views. Supervisors should provide information and feedback, but they also need to be good listeners, questioning and probing to determine the reasons behind the teacher's decisions and actions.

Supervisory Styles

It has been suggested that a supervisor needs a wide range of styles in order to work with teachers at various stages of development. Hersey and Blanchard (1977) have defined such a range of styles. In order to understand the scope of these styles, it is necessary to clarify Hersey and Blanchard's use of the terms "task behavior" and "relationship behavior." Task behavior refers to the supervisor defining the job, making decisions unilaterally, giving directions, letting the teacher know what is expected, and providing close supervision. Relationship behavior, on the other hand, provides the teacher with a share in the decision making, along with friendly interaction, recognition, psychological "strokes," and emotional support. The four styles defined by Hersey and Blanchard are as follows:

1. High-task/low-relationship behavior is referred to as "telling" because this style is characterized by one-way communication in which the leader defines the role of the followers and tells them what, how, when, and where to do various tasks.
2. High-task/high-relationship behavior is referred to as "selling" because with this style most of the direction is still provided by the leader. He or she also attempts through two-way communication and emotional support to get the follower or followers to buy into decisions that have to be made.
3. High-relationship/low-task behavior is called "participating" because the leader and follower or followers share in decision-making through two-way communication. The leader shows a great deal of facilitating behavior, because he or she recognizes that the follower or followers have the ability and knowledge to do the task.
4. Low-relationship/low-task behavior is labeled "delegating" because the style entails letting the follower or followers "run their own show" through delegation and with only light supervision, since they are considered to be high in both task and psychological maturity.

It is important to remember that Hersey and Blanchard are not specifically concerned with educational management but rather with management principles in general. It is hard to imagine, for example, a circumstance in education where one would use high task/low-relationship. This particular style may be appropriate in crisis situations such as those faced by the military or firefighters, but they are not usually appropriate in working with teachers. A possible exception may be where things are so totally out of control that the safety of students is in jeopardy.

It is easy to see, however, that high-task/high-relationship would be especially appropriate when working with young teachers lacking fundamental skills and know-how, while management that is based on low-task approaches would be called for with experienced teachers whose performance is exemplary. Low-relationship/low-task may in fact often be a style well suited to this latter category—in many cases the last thing exemplary teachers want is for a supervisor to get in their way by trying to be helpful.

Another consideration when using these styles is that task and relationship behaviors lie on a continuum. It is not a matter of always using either high- or low-task or relationships; many degrees exist in between. In the hands of a skilled supervisor, it usually becomes a matter of knowing when and why to increase or decrease either component in order to get the desired results.

The relationship component can be a special problem. It has two basic dimensions: that of collaborative, shared decision making and that of friendly interaction and emotional support. It is usually the collaborative dimension that is adjusted when working with teachers. Supervisors may withhold friendly interaction and emotional support in some management settings, but they must exercise care when attempting this technique with teachers; it can easily become counterproductive. Also, supervisors should avoid using one particular type of shared decision making: making the decision and then "sharing" it with the teacher.

Any style can be effective or ineffective. What works in one situation may not work in another. The job of the supervisor is to know the appropriate style to use with a particular teacher in a particular situation. For example, Teacher A is doing reasonably well at attracting and holding students in the program. The students, however, are not learning fundamental skills, and the ensemble's performance at concerts and adjudications is below district standards. Teachers like this lack the technical knowledge and skills to get the job done but do not recognize their deficiencies. They want to do a good job, think they are doing a good job, but are not.

Many supervisors use a low-task/low-relationship approach with teachers such as Teacher A. By more or less ignoring poor performance, they allow it to continue. The first step in helping this teacher improve is to open communication channels. Without this, no improvement can be expected. The next step is to initiate task behavior and make sure the teacher is aware of expected standards of performance. After helping set long-range and interim goals, the supervisor should observe the teacher carefully to identify problems and to diagnose and prescribe solutions for those problems. As improvement occurs, task behavior can be reduced and positive reinforcement given for improved performance.

Teacher B is not attracting and holding students in the program. If this persists, there will be no program at the succeeding level. The few students in Teacher B's class do acquire fundamental performance skills. Teacher B has the ability but lacks the willingness to take responsibility for getting results and seems lackadaisical and unmotivated.

Assume that Teacher B and the supervisor have known each other for many years and are former teaching colleagues. The supervisor has maintained high-relationship/low-task behaviors, which have probably been viewed as permissiveness. In working with Teacher B, it would be best to keep the communication channels open. At the same time, the supervisor should take care not to let the friendly interaction dimension of relationship behavior get too high until the teacher begins to take some responsibility for attracting and holding students. Tasks designed to increase the number of students in the program need to be spelled out, and Teacher B should be encouraged to capitalize on teaching strengths and formulate strategies for self-improvement. Relationship behavior should be gradually increased as improvement occurs, and task behavior correspondingly diminished.

Teacher C is a beginning teacher. Teacher C wants to be liked by the students, who are taking advantage of this. Classroom control in beginning band is deteriorating. In order to keep the students interested and motivated, Teacher C has slighted teaching the fundamentals of attitude, breathing, air flow, and embouchure, and proceeded immediately to the method book, through which he is moving at an alarming rate. The supervisor hardly knows Teacher C, but was impressed at the time of hiring and believes that this teacher is capable of improving and becoming an effective instructor.

Because the supervisor and Teacher C are new to each other, the supervisor must first open the communication channels. The supervisor needs to emphasize task accomplishment and to make sure that the district's expectations are clear. Definite and attainable goals must then be set. The supervisor must be accessible to Teacher C, and must ensure that appropriate help is provided. While supervising closely, the supervisor needs to be as supportive and encouraging as possible. Positive reinforcement along with psychological "strokes" and friendly interaction should be provided as improvement occurs.

Conclusion of the Conference

At the conclusion of a conference, several possible courses of action exist. If the evaluation calendar specifies additional conferences, and if the supervisor finds that the teacher is performing in a satisfactory manner and has only normal growth and improvement needs, then preliminary plans for the next observation should be discussed. If this is the final scheduled observation and conference (and if the teacher is performing satisfactorily), then the written conclusions from this and similar conferences held during the year will serve as the basis for the final written evaluation (see Appendix E). Where the supervisor notes serious deficiencies in performance, the teacher will, at this point in the evaluation process, be placed on a plan of assistance.

VII. Plans of Assistance

Sometimes efforts to help teachers grow and improve are ineffective or inadequate, and a teacher's deficiencies go beyond normal growth and improvement needs. Such deficiencies, unless they are remedied, eventually become grounds for dismissal. If a teacher has deficiencies of this type, a plan of assistance is called for (see Appendix F).

Specifics of the Plan of Assistance

Attachments are necessary when using this form, because not enough space is provided to write in sufficient information under each item. The items may be explained as follows.

Description of Deficiency

The items listed here will usually come from the job descriptions or standards. The most common deficiencies are poor classroom control, lack of appropriate and effective instructional feedback, and inability to attract and hold a sufficient number of students.

Supervisor's Expectancies

This is simply a description of how things should look after the deficiency has been corrected. A close relationship exists between these statements and those in the "Description of Deficiency" category. If lack of appropriate and effective instructional feedback is the problem, the supervisor's expectancies would likely include statements such as "after the deficiency is corrected, the teacher will accurately identify problems in the fundamentals of musical performance, including tone quality, intonation, balance, and rhythmic style and accuracy, and he or she will suggest and employ corrective procedures resulting in a satisfactory level of performance."

Recommended Program to Correct Deficiency

The program may take various forms depending upon the deficiency. Some components that have been used successfully in remedial programs are (1) observations by the supervisor and others; (2) videotaping classes, followed by a debriefing; (3) visiting other teachers and observing their classes; (4) observing model lessons taught by the supervisor or others; (5) taking private lessons on voice or instrument; (6) taking university courses such as conducting or classroom management; and (7) taking in-service classes provided by the local district. Supervisors can often arrange to teach or have someone else teach such courses, as, for example, beginning string or vocal techniques, for college credit.

Criteria That Will Be Used to Measure Correction

This part of the form can be completed by taking the statements appearing under the heading "Supervisor's Expectancies" and writing specific indicators for them. If, for example, reference is made there to the supervisor's expectation that the classroom environment will be orderly and supportive, the criteria to measure the correction may include the statements that (1) few, if any, reprimands will be necessary to maintain control; (2) little or no off-task behavior will take place; (3) students will make a minimum of unsolicited off-task comments; (4) students will be concentrating; (5) the facial expressions and body language of students will reflect interest and involvement; and (6) the class will move quickly from one activity to another, with control maintained and little time lost in transition.

Assistance and Resources to Be Provided

The entries under this category should spring from the "recommended program" category. The services provided by the supervisor, other administrators, or resource persons should be listed here. The district should pay for any classes, lessons, and resource persons.

Monitoring Procedures

The number and scheduling of observations and conferences should be explicitly stated. If activities other than these are included in the plan, they should also be noted. Moreover, if some monitoring is to be done by individuals other than the supervisor, that should be specified in writing.

Date by Which the Plan Must Be Completed

Reasonable and sufficient time for satisfactory completion must be allowed. If possible, the teacher should agree to the date that appears here.

The decision to place a teacher on a plan of assistance is usually made by the supervisor who has been working closely with the teacher on efforts to grow and improve. Upon successful completion of the plan of assistance, the teacher is returned to the normal evaluation cycle (see figure 1.1). If the plan of assistance is not completed successfully, the teacher will be placed on what is called an "intensive plan of assistance" (see Appendix G). This amounts to a second chance for the teacher, and is required by law in some states. According to Acheson (1982), districts that have used plans of assistance "report that about half of the teachers are successful in making a satisfactory improvement. Half of the others resign, and the rest are non-renewed" (p. 67).

When instituting a plan of assistance or an intensive plan of assistance, it should be kept in mind that the growth and improvement of the teacher is still the top priority, and every effort should be made to help the teacher complete the plan successfully. This is true even if the supervisor questions whether the teacher is likely to be successful. The administration of plans of assistance is usually the responsibility of the supervisor. Nonetheless, it is a good idea to have another administrator involved. The building principal would, of course, be the obvious choice. Some districts use a committee to monitor the progress of the plan. Such a committee may include the music supervisor, another administrator (preferably a building principal), and, if teachers are permitted to serve, another music teacher. Sometimes, as in the Salt Lake City plan (Williams et al. 1981), the teacher being evaluated is permitted to choose another teacher as an additional member.

The first step in developing a plan of assistance is to notify the teacher in writing that he or she is being placed on a plan of assistance. Some districts have plan-of-assistance forms that include a statement to this effect (see Appendixes F and G). Where such a form exists, a separate letter of notice is not necessary.

Developing the Plan of Assistance

The next step is to develop the plan itself. This should be done in consultation, as distinguished from collaboration, with the teacher. The distinction is important. Consultation means that the remedial plan is thoroughly discussed and the teacher's views are sought and that agreements are made on the timetable. The supervisor, however, takes the lead and is directive. In the regular evaluation cycle for growth and improvement, the method of operation is usually more collaborative.

The supervisor needs to remember the following points when working with a teacher on a plan of assistance.

Changing Behavior

Behavior is not easy to change. Speaking of the relative difficulty of changing individuals' knowledge, attitude, or behavior, Hersey and Blanchard (1977) state that

> changes in knowledge are the easiest to make, followed by changes in attitudes. Attitude structures differ from knowledge structures in that they are

emotionally charged in a positive or negative way. Changes in behavior are significantly more difficult and time-consuming than either of the previous two levels. (p. 2)

As Thomas Friedman (2005) has said, "People don't change when you tell them they should. They change when they tell themselves they must" (p. 462). The job of the supervisor, then, is to recognize the kind of change that is desired and to structure the remedial plan accordingly.

Competence and Motivation

In most cases, unsatisfactory performance stems from either a competence problem or a motivational problem. Deficient performance is usually a case of a teacher who is willing but not able, or who is able but not willing. The latter cases are the most difficult. An example would be the instrumental teacher with low numbers of students for whom outside playing activities have a higher priority than building a program. A plan of assistance for such a teacher would likely include very specific, goal-oriented recruiting activities to be carried out with demonstrated results.

Are performance deficiencies competence problems or motivational problems? Teacher competence is not the real question; teacher performance is. A teacher can be competent but fail in getting the job done because of lack of energy or a motivational problem. It is important, therefore, to focus on performance results rather than competence. Also, it is difficult to try to prove that someone is incompetent; it is much easier to substantiate the fact that they are not getting the job done. This requires, of course, that the job be carefully defined in standards and job descriptions.

Improvement and Performance

Improvement on a plan of assistance does not necessarily mean that the teacher has become a satisfactory performer. The teacher may have come only part way on the continuum stretching from his or her original performance level to the district's standard for satisfactory performance.

Just a little improvement is not enough, nor is marginal performance enough. The teacher *must* become a satisfactory performer, as anything short of this is a disservice to students. Upon completion of a plan of assistance, the teacher will or will not be capable of providing the high-quality experiences students deserve in the music program. This must be decided by the supervisor or the evaluation committee.

Documentation

Documentation is extremely important in a plan of assistance. The plan, along with records of monitoring and observations, must be kept in writing and copies must be given to the teacher. Failure to do this may legally compromise a termination, should that be the outcome of an unsatisfactory plan completion. Acheson (1982) has summarized other aspects of teacher evaluation that, if not properly handled, may compromise termination:

Goals: were they reasonable, fair, clear?
Observations: were they systematic, unbiased, expert?
Evaluations (formal reports): were they capricious, vindictive, inconsistent?
District standards: are they justifiable, well-informed, reasonable?
Programs of assistance: were they provided, helpful, and followed up? (p. 84)

VIII. A Final Word

Being an effective supervisor has been compared to being an effective teacher. In the same way that teachers use a wide variety of teaching skills to help all kinds of students grow and learn, the supervisor uses a wide repertoire of evaluation skills to help all kinds of teachers grow and improve. Teachers learn a great deal about their teaching skills from observing and interacting with their students. In like manner, supervisors also learn much about their skills as evaluators from the teachers with whom they are working. Mrs. Anna's declaration in *The King and I,* "by your students you'll be taught," was never more true than when applied to supervisors and teachers working together in the evaluation process.

Teachers, however, do not constitute the supervisor's primary concern. Supervisors must look beyond teacher considerations to their ultimate responsibility: to guarantee students the finest musical experiences possible. The supervisor should always keep in mind that the lowest performing teacher in a school district is the standard-bearer for that program. This is because the level of performance of that teacher is what the supervisor is willing to accept. This is, indeed, a scary thought. In the end, it's not how much is known about evaluation that matters. It's what's done about it.

Endnotes

Acheson, K. A. (1982). *Techniques in the evaluation of teachers.* Salem, OR: Confederation of Oregon School Administrators.

Acheson, K. A., & Gall, M. D. (1987). *Techniques in the clinical supervision of teachers: Preservice and in-service applications* (2nd ed.). New York: Longman.

Acheson, K. A., & Gall, M. D. (1997). *Techniques in the clinical supervision of teachers* (4th ed.). New York: Longman.

Baxter, S. G., & Stauffer, S. L. (1988). Music teaching: A review of common practice. In C. Fowler (Ed.), *The Crane Symposium: Toward an understanding of teaching and learning of music performance* (pp. 49–61). Potsdam: Potsdam College of the State University of New York.

Blumberg, A., & Cusick, P. (1970). Supervisor-teacher interaction: An analysis of verbal behavior. *Education* 91: 126–134.

Brophy, J. E., & Evertson, C. M. (1976). *Learning from teaching: A developmental perspective.* Boston: Allyn and Bacon.

Cutietta, R. (1986). Performance isn't a dirty word. *Music Educators Journal* 73(1): 18–22.

Drucker, P. F. (1964). *Managing for results.* New York: Harper & Row.

Eisner, E. W. (1979). The qualitative forms of evaluation for improving educational practice. *Educational Evaluation and Policy Analysis* 1(6): 11–19.

Friedman, T. L. (2005). *The world is flat.* New York: Farrar, Straus and Giroux.

George, W. E., Hoffer, C. R., Lehman, P. R., & Taylor, R. G. (Eds.). (1986). *The school music program: Description and standards* (2nd ed.). Reston, VA: MENC (The National Association for Music Education).

Griffith, F. (1975). *A handbook for the observation of teaching and learning.* Midland, MI: Pendell.

Hersey, P., & Blanchard K. H. (1977). *Management of organizational behavior: Utilizing human resources* (3rd ed.). Englewood Cliffs, NJ: Prentice-Hall.

Joint Committee on Standards for Educational Evaluation. (1988). *The personnel evaluation standards: How to assess systems of evaluating educators.* Newbury Park, CA: Sage.

Kounin, J. S. (1970). *Discipline and group management in classrooms*. New York: Holt, Rinehart, & Winston.

Lehman, P. R. (Ed.). (1994). *The school music program: A new vision*. Reston, VA: MENC (The National Association for Music Education).

Lehman, P. R. (Ed.). (1996). *Performance standards for music grades PreK–12: Strategies and benchmarks for assessing progress toward the national standards*. Reston, VA: MENC (The National Association for Music Education).

McNergney, R. F., & Medley, D. M. (1984). Teacher evaluation. In J. M. Cooper (Ed.), *Developing skills for instructional supervision* (pp. 147–178). New York: Longman.

Neidig, K. (1979). An interview with John Paynter. *The Instrumentalist* 33 (12): 10–17.

Revelli, W. (n.d.). *Inside a live rehearsal: A bands of America workshop, featuring Dr. William Revelli* [video]. (Available from Sharper Video Productions, Palatine, IL.)

Rosenshine, B. V. (1979). Content, time, and direct instruction. In P. L. Peterson & H. J. Walberg (Eds.), *Research on teaching: Concepts, findings, and implications* (pp. 28–56). Berkeley, CA: McCutchan.

Shavelson, R. J., & Stern, P. D. (1981). Research on teachers' pedagogical thoughts, judgments, decisions, and behavior. *Review of Educational Research* 51: 455–498.

Taylor, P. H. (1970). *How teachers plan their courses*. London: National Foundation for Educational Research in England and Wales.

Weber, J. R. (1987). *Teacher evaluation as a strategy for improving instruction*. Eugene: University of Oregon. ED 287213

Williams, D. A., Coppola, V., Howard, L., Huck, J., King, P., & Monroe, S. (1981, April 27). Teachers are in trouble. *Newsweek*, 78–84.

Zahorik, J. A. (1975). Teachers' planning models. *Educational Leadership* 33: 134–139.

Appendix A
Performance Goal Planning Form

Performance Goal Planning Form

Goal No. _____ of _____

Staff Member's Name_____ Probationary _____

School _____ . Temporary _____

Assignment _____ Permanent _____

I. Performance goal statement:

II. Activities planned for goal accomplishment:

III. Monitoring procedures:
(Include activities/techniques/procedures for measuring goal accomplishment. Also include projected dates, where appropriate, by which monitoring will occur.)

IV. General evaluation criterion or job description/standard item to which this goal is related:

V. The projected date of completion for this goal is:

Staff Member's Signature_____ Date _____

Supervisor's Signature _____ Date _____

This form may be photocopied for classes or other groups.

Appendix B

Pre-observation Form

Pre-observation Form

Staff Member _____ Supervisor _____

Date and Time of Visit _____ Subject or Class _____

I. Objective(s) of the lesson

II. Instructional procedures to be used

III. How student achievement of objectives will be assessed

IV. Specific areas for observation

V. Type of data collection to be used

VI. Other information needed by observer

Staff Member's Signature _____ Date _____

Supervisor's Signature _____ Date _____

This form may be photocopied for classes or other groups.

Appendix C

Observation Guide

Observation Guide

A. Quality of the classroom environment
  1. Is the classroom task oriented, yet relaxed?
  2. Is the teacher continuously aware of everything going on?
  3. Is the environment productive?
  4. Is there a seriousness of purpose?
  5. Does the teacher vary the intensity level, or is there a sameness to the class?
  6. Is there evidence of planning?
  7. Are routines and procedures well-established?
  8. Are students actively participating and enjoying the class?
  9. Is there an absence of indiscriminate playing and talking during instruction?
  10. Is there a shared sense of accomplishment?
  11. Do students take pride in what they're doing?
  12. Are students concentrating?
  13. Do students evaluate their own efforts and progress, and take some responsibility for their own learning?
  14. Do students show respect for one another and for the teacher?
B. Quality of teacher-student interaction
  1. Is there an absence of negative affect: put-downs, sarcasm, and the like?
  2. Is the teacher supportive and encouraging?
  3. Does the teacher react with sensitivity to the students' needs and feelings?
  4. Is there an absence of off-task comments by students, such as "Why do we have to do this?"
  5. Do facial and body language reflect concentration, interest, and enthusiasm as opposed to boredom and frustration?
C. Quality of Instruction
  1. Does the teacher give clear instructions? Do the students know what is expected?
  2. Does the teacher practice "preventive medicine" by careful teaching of fundamentals in order to avoid future problems?
  3. Does the teacher demonstrate effective use of diagnostic and prescriptive procedures? Does the teacher:
    a. Recognize when something is wrong?
    b. Find the problem?
    c. Prescribe and try a solution?
    d. Persist until the problem is fixed, or leave it by design and not by default?

4. Does the teacher present instruction, provide corrective feedback, and reinforce instruction on the following?
   a. Individual and group performance skills:

Breathing	Intonation
Position	Rhythm (accuracy)
Tone quality	Rhythm (style)
Balance and definition of parts	Articulation
Phrasing and expressiveness	Fingerings
Style	Bowing
Dynamics	Vowels
Technique	Focus
Embouchure	Diction

   b. Other learning outcomes:

Scales	Phrase relationships
Intervals	Antecedent
Chords	Consequent
Key relationships	Variation
Major and minor	Sequential
Modulation	Historical considerations
Cadences	Major forms, styles, and genre
Contrapuntal devices	

D. Teacher behaviors. Does the teacher:
   1. Have high standards and expectations and demonstrate an inner desire for excellence?
   2. Show enthusiasm?
   3. Have an emotionally flat style, or is the energy and intensity level varied to correspond to the instructional context?
   4. Know the music?
   5. Maintain good eye contact?
   6. Take responsibility for getting results?
   7. Do more than just mention corrective procedures, and show persistence until results are achieved? (Instruction must be substantive—that is, more than saying "Open your mouth," "Watch the dynamics," "Tenors are flat," or "Breathe from the diaphragm.")

Appendix D

Post-observation Form

Post-observation Form

Staff Member _____ Supervisor _____

Date and Time of Visit _____ Subject or Class _____

I. Analysis of lesson

II. Conclusions discussed

III. Plans for next observation

Staff Member's Signature_____ Date _____

Supervisor's Signature _____ Date _____

This form may be photocopied for classes or other groups.

Appendix E

Teacher Evaluation Form

Teacher Evaluation Form

Name _____   Employee Status _____

Assignment _____   School _____

General instructions: This evaluation is based on the individual's performance goals and the district's job description(s) and standards. Use
the reverse side or additional pages as needed.

1. In what ways has the teacher met, failed to meet, or exceeded the performance goals, standards, and job description?

2. In what areas has the teacher shown development and growth in the
   teaching profession?

3. In what specific areas does the teacher need to demonstrate additional development and growth?

4. Four-point Rating Scale:* (circle one item)

Performance Exceeds Expectations	The performance of the teacher exceeds required responsibilities, consistently producing exemplary work that optimizes student achievement and behavior.
Performance Meets Expectations	The performance of the teacher consistently fulfills responsibilities, resulting in quality work that impacts student achievement or behavior in a positive manner. *This rating is a high performance criterion and is expected of all teachers.*
Performance Needs Improvement	The teacher inconsistently meets responsibilities, resulting in less than quality work performance and poor student results or behavior.

| Performance Is Unsatisfactory | The teacher does not adequately fulfill responsibilities, resulting in inferior work performance and negatively impacting student achievement or behavior. |

5. Supervisor's recommendations:

Continuation of employment _____

Termination of Employment _____

Other _____

Comments: (use additional pages)
6. Teacher's response, if desired [as provided by law].
7. The following attachments are a part of this report:

This is to certify that we have read and discussed the above report:

Staff Member's Signature _____ Date _____

Supervisor's Signature _____ Date _____

*Four-point Rating Scale. Used by permission from J. H. Stronge and P. D. Tucker, *Handbook on teacher evaluation: Assessing and improving performance* (Larchmont, NY: Eye on Education, 2003).

This form may be photocopied for classes or other groups.

Appendix F

Plan of Assistance

Plan of Assistance

Name _____ Probationary _____

School _____ Temporary _____

Assignment _____ Permanent _____

You are being placed on this Plan of Assistance because of unsatisfactory performance as specified in the deficiencies identified below. This plan is designed to help you correct those deficiencies. Upon successful completion of the plan, you will be returned to the regular evaluation program. If the plan is not successfully completed, you will be placed on an "Intensive Plan of Assistance."

I. Description of deficiency
   (Cite related standards or job description items)

II. Supervisor's expectancies
   (How things should look after the deficiency has been corrected)

III. Recommended program to correct deficiency

IV. Criteria that will be used to measure correction

V. Assistance and resources to be provided

VI. Monitoring procedures

VII.   Date by which plan must be completed

Staff Member's Signature_____ Date _____

Supervisor's Signature _____ Date _____

This form may be photocopied for classes or other groups.

Appendix G

Intensive Plan of Assistance

Intensive Plan of Assistance

Name _____ Probationary _____

School _____ Temporary _____

Assignment _____ Permanent _____

You are being placed on this Intensive Plan of Assistance because the Plan of Assistance dated _____ was not successfully completed, and your performance continues to be unsatisfactory with respect to the deficiencies identified below. You will be returned to the regular evaluation program upon successful completion of this plan.

I. Description of deficiency
    (Cite related standards or job description items)

II. Supervisor's expectancies
    (How things should look after the deficiency has been corrected)

III. Recommended program to correct deficiency

IV. Criteria that will be used to measure correction

V. Assistance and resources to be provided

VI. Monitoring procedures

VII. Date by which plan must completed

Staff Member's Signature_____ Date _____

Supervisor's Signature _____ Date _____

This form may be photocopied for classes or other groups .

Appendix H
Resources

The National Standards for Music and Related Resources, published by MENC, available from Rowman & Littlefield:

Benchmarks in action: A guide to standards-based assessment in music. Project editor, Carolynn Lindeman. 2003.

Opportunity-to-learn standards for music instruction: Grades PreK–12. 1994.

Performing with understanding: The challenge of the national standards for music education, edited by Bennett Reimer. 2000.

Performance standards for music: Strategies and benchmarks for assessing progress toward the national standards, grades PreK–12. Chairman, Paul R. Lehman. 1996.

The school music program—a new vision: The K–12 national standards, PreK standards, and what they mean to music educators. Chairman, Paul R. Lehman. 1994.

Teaching examples: Ideas for music educators. Project director, Paul R. Lehman. 1994.

Also published by MENC and available from Rowman & Littlefield Education: Strategies for Teaching Series, Carolynn A. Lindeman, series editor.

Strategies for teaching elementary and middle-level chorus, compiled and edited by Ann Roberts Small and Judy K. Bowers. 1997.

Strategies for teaching high school chorus, compiled and edited by Randal Swiggum. 1998.

Strategies for teaching strings and orchestra, compiled and edited by Dorothy A. Straub, Louis S. Bergonzi, and Anne C. Witt. 1996.

Strategies for teaching beginning and intermediate band, compiled and edited by Edward J. Kvet and Janet M. Tweed. 1996.

Strategies for teaching high school band, compiled and edited by Edward J. Kvet and John E. Williamson. 1998.

Other Selected Resources for Teaching Music Through Performance:

Buchanan, H. J., & Mehaffey, M. W. (Eds.). (2005). *Teaching music through performance in choir* (Vol. 1). Chicago: GIA Publications.

Garofalo, R. J. (1992). *Guides to masterworks* (Vol. 1). Ft. Lauderdale, FL: Meredith Music Publications.

Garofalo, R. J. (1995). *Guides to masterworks* (Vol. 2). Ft. Lauderdale, FL: Meredith Music Publications.

Labuta, J. A. (1997). *Teaching musicianship in the high school band* (Rev. ed.). Ft. Lauderdale, FL: Meredith Music Publications.

Littrell, D. (2003). *Teaching music through performance in orchestra* (Vol. 2). Chicago: GIA Publications.

Littrell, D., & Racin, L. (Eds.). (2001). *Teaching music through performance in orchestra.* Chicago: GIA Publications.

Miles, R. (Ed.). (1997–2004). *Teaching music through performance in band* (Vols. 1–5). Chicago: GIA Publications.

Miles, R., & Dvorak, T. (Eds.). (2001). *Teaching music through performance in beginning band.* Chicago: GIA Publications.

O'Toole, P. (2003). *Shaping sound musicians.* Chicago: GIA Publications.

Whitlock, R. (1982). *Choral insights, general edition.* San Diego, CA: Neil A. Kjos Music Company.

Whitlock, R. (1982). *Choral insights, renaissance edition* (L. Anderson, Ed.). San Diego, CA: Neil A. Kjos Music Company.

Whitlock, R. (1985). *Choral insights, baroque edition* (L. Anderson, Ed.). San Diego, CA: Neil A. Kjos Music Company.

Whitlock, R. (1990). *Choral insights, classical edition* (L. Anderson, Ed.). San Diego, CA: Neil A. Kjos Music Company.

Bibliography

Acheson, K. A. (1982). *Techniques in the evaluation of teachers.* Salem, OR: Confederation of Oregon School Administrators.

Acheson, K. A., & Gall, M. D. (1987). *Techniques in the clinical supervision of teachers: Preservice and in-service applications* (2nd ed.). New York: Longman.

Acheson, K. A., & Gall, M. D. (1997). *Techniques in the clinical supervision of teachers* (4th ed.). New York: Longman.

Baxter, S. G., & Stauffer, S. L. (1988). Music teaching: A review of common practice. In C. Fowler (Ed.), *The Crane Symposium: Toward an understanding of teaching and learning of music performance* (pp. 49–61). Potsdam: Potsdam College of the State University of New York.

Berliner, D. C. (1980). Using research on teaching for the improvement of classroom practice. *Theory Into Practice* 19: 302–308.

Blumberg, A., & Cusick, P. (1970). Supervisor-teacher interaction: An analysis of verbal behavior. *Education* 91: 126–134.

Brophy, J. E. (1979). *Advances in teacher effectiveness research* (Occasional Paper No. 18). East Lansing: Michigan State University, Institute for Research on Teaching.

Brophy, J. E., & Evertson, C. M. (1976). *Learning from teaching: A developmental perspective.* Boston: Allyn and Bacon.

Clark, C. M., & Yinger, R. J. (1979). Teachers' thinking. In P. L. Peterson & H. J. Walberg (Eds.), *Research on teaching: Concepts, findings, and implications* (pp. 231–263). Berkeley: McCutchan.

Cutietta, R. (1986). Performance isn't a dirty word. *Music Educators Journal* 73(1): 18–22.

Darling-Hammond, L. (1990). Teacher evaluation in transition: Emerging roles and evolving methods. In J. Millman & L. Darling-Hammond (Eds.), *The new handbook of teacher evaluation* (pp. 17–32). Newbury Park, CA: Sage.

Darling-Hammond, L. (1999). *Teacher quality and student achievement: A review of state policy evidence.* Seattle: Center for the Study of Teaching and Policy, University of Washington.

Doyle, K. O., Jr. (1983). *Evaluating teaching.* Lexington, MA: Heath.

Drucker, P. F. (1964). *Managing for results.* New York: Harper & Row.

Duke, R. A. (1999/2000). Measures of instructional effectiveness in music research. *Bulletin of the Council for Research in Music Education* 143: 1–48.

Eisner, E. W. (1979). The qualitative forms of evaluation for improving educational practice. *Educational Evaluation and Policy Analysis* 1(6): 11–19.

Eisner, E. W. (1982). An artistic approach to supervision. In T. J. Sergiovanni (Ed.), *Supervision of teaching* (pp. 53–66). Alexandria, VA: Association for Supervision and Curriculum Development.

Fisher, C. W., Berliner, D. C., Filby, N. N., Marliane, R., Cahen, L. S., Dishaw, M. M., & Moore, J. E. (1978). *Beginning teacher evaluation study: Phase III-B: A summary of the final report.* San Francisco: State Commission for Teacher Preparation and Licensing.

Friedman, T. L. (2005). *The world is flat.* New York: Farrar, Straus & Giroux.

Gage, N. L. (1978). The yield of research on teaching. *Phi Delta Kappan* 60: 229–235.

George, W. E., Hoffer, C. R., Lehman, P. R., & Taylor, R. G. (Eds.). (1986). *The school music program: Description and standards* (2nd ed.). Reston, VA: MENC (The National Association for Music Education).

Grant, J. W., & Drafall, L. E. (1991). Teacher effectiveness research: A review and comparison. *Bulletin of the Council for Research in Music Education* 108: 31–48.

Griffith, F. (1975). *A handbook for the observation of teaching and learning.* Midland, MI: Pendell.

Hersey, P., & Blanchard K. H. (1977). *Management of organizational behavior: Utilizing human resources* (3rd ed.). Englewood Cliffs, NJ: Prentice-Hall.

Joint Committee on Standards for Educational Evaluation. (1988). *The personnel evaluation standards: How to assess systems of evaluating educators.* Newbury Park, CA: Sage.

Kounin, J. S. (1970). *Discipline and group management in classrooms.* New York: Holt, Rinehart, & Winston.

Lehman, P. R. (Ed.). (1994). *The school music program: A new vision.* Reston, VA: MENC (The National Association for Music Education).

Lehman, P. R. (Ed.). (1996). *Performance standards for music grades PreK–12: Strategies and benchmarks for assessing progress toward the national standards.* Reston, VA: MENC (The National Association for Music Education).

Lindeman, C. A. (Ed.). (2003). *Benchmarks in action: A guide to standards-based assessment in music.* Reston, VA: MENC (The National Association for Music Education).

McNergney, R. F., & Medley, D. M. (1984). Teacher evaluation. In J. M. Cooper (Ed.), *Developing skills for instructional supervision* (pp. 147–178). New York: Longman.

Medley, D. M. (1979). The effectiveness of teachers. In P. L. Peterson & H. J. Walberg (Eds.), *Research on teaching: Concepts, findings, and implications* (pp. 11–27). Berkeley, CA: McCutchan.

National Board for Professional Teaching Standards. (1994). *What teachers should know and be able to do.* Detroit, MI: Author.

National Commission on Excellence in Education. (1983). *A nation at risk: The imperative for educational reform.* Washington, DC: Author.

National Commission on Teaching and America's Future. (1996). *What matters most: Teaching for America's future.* New York: Author.

Neidig, K. (1979). An interview with John Paynter. *The Instrumentalist* 33 (12): 10–17.

O'Toole, P. (2003). *Shaping sound musicians: An innovative approach to teaching comprehensive musicianship through performance.* Chicago: GIA Publications, Inc.

Price, H. E. (1983). The effect of conductor academic task presentation, conductor reinforcement, and ensemble practice on performers' musical achievement, attentiveness, and attitude. *Journal of Research in Music Education* 31: 245–258.

Revelli, W. (n.d.). *Inside a live rehearsal: A bands of America workshop, featuring Dr. William Revelli* [video]. (Available from Sharper Video Productions, Palatine, IL.)

Rosenshine, B. V. (1979). Content, time, and direct instruction. In P. L. Peterson & H. J. Walberg (Eds.), *Research on teaching: Concepts, findings, and implications* (pp. 28–56). Berkeley, CA: McCutchan.

Sang, R. C. (1982). *Modified path analysis of a skills-based instructional effectiveness model for beginning teachers in instrumental music education.* Unpublished doctoral dissertation, University of Michigan, Ann Arbor.

Sang, R. C. (1987). A study of the relationship between instrumental music teachers' modeling skills and pupil performance behaviors. *Bulletin of the Council for Research in Music Education* 91: 155–159.

Shavelson, R. J., & Stern, P. D. (1981). Research on teachers' pedagogical thoughts, judgments, decisions, and behavior. *Review of Educational Research* 51: 455–498.

Stronge, J. H., & Tucker, P. D. (2003). *Handbook on teacher evaluation: Assessing and improving performance.* Larchmont, NY: Eye on Education.

Taebel, D. K. (1992). The evaluation of music teachers and teaching. In R. J. Colwell (Ed.), *Handbook of research on music teaching and learning* (pp. 310–329). New York: Schirmer Books.

Taylor, P. H. (1970). *How teachers plan their courses.* London: National Foundation for Educational Research in England and Wales.

Tucker, P. D., & Stronge, J. H. (2005). *Linking teacher evaluation and student learning.* Alexandria, VA: Association for Supervision and Curriculum Development.

Weber, J. R. (1987). *Teacher evaluation as a strategy for improving instruction.* Eugene: University of Oregon (ERIC Clearinghouse on Educational Management). ED 287213

Williams, D. A., Coppola, V., Howard, L., Huck, J., King, P., & Monroe, S. (1981, April 27). Teachers are in trouble. *Newsweek,* 78–84.

Zahorik, J. A. (1975). Teachers' planning models. *Educational Leadership* 33: 134–139.

About the Author

David P. Doerksen is a retired chair of the Music Education Department at the University of Oregon School of Music. He has taught instrumental and vocal music to students from elementary through university level. Before going to the University of Oregon in 1983, he was supervisor of music for the Salem, Oregon, public schools for nine years. During his tenure there, Salem was listed among MENC's exemplary programs. Dr. Doerksen holds degrees from Willamette University, the University of Southern California, and the University of Oregon, and serves as a consultant in teacher evaluation and curriculum development.